SPIRITUAL WARFARE

A COMPREHENSIVE GUIDE TO
PERSONAL HEALING AND DELIVERANCE

Dr. Jerry Piscopo
Dr. Sherill Piscopo
with
Simon and Trish Presland

SPIRITUAL WARFARE
A COMPREHENSIVE GUIDE TO
PERSONAL HEALING AND DELIVERANCE
by Drs. Jerry & Sherill Piscopo
with Simon and Trish Presland

ISBN: 1461012783
ISBN-13: 9781461012788

Copies of this book may be ordered through
booksellers online or by contacting

Drs. Jerry & Sherill Piscopo
28491 Utica Road, Roseville, MI 48066
586-773-6568
www.evangel-churches.com
or
Simon and Trish Presland
www.thewritechoice.org

Endorsements

Drs. Jerry and Sherill Piscopo have blessed the Body of Christ by sharing their lives and ministry of deliverance and inner healing. They do not speak from book learning alone but from actual experience in bringing inner healing and deliverance to thousands over the last twenty-five years. The truths and practices presented are biblically based. The fruit of their ministry proves the Holy Spirit is involved in their lives and ministry. Every Christian and ordained minister needs to read this book to gain greater ability to bring inner healing to oneself and to God's people.

Dr. Bill Hamon
Bishop of Christian International Ministries Network (CIMN) and
best-selling author

For years, I have watched in wonder as Drs. Jerry and Sherill Piscopo have passionately championed the needs of the oppressed and bound in the church and in the world. *Spiritual Warfare A Comprehensive Guide to Personal Healing and Deliverance*, is a masterwork of all they believe and teach so effectively. Decades of experience combined with a rare grasp of the Scriptures have prepared the Piscopos to equip your life and inspire your faith as few others can. If you are tired of being held back and are ready to be a vessel of healing and freedom in the hands of the Lord, I recommend this book to you.

Dr. David Cannistraci
GateWay City Church
San Jose, California

Drs. Jerry and Sherill Piscopo have written a valuable book for the Body of Christ in their book *Spiritual Warfare A Comprehensive Guide to Personal Healing and Deliverance*. Many have written about this or that aspect of inner healing or deliverance. What has been missing are enough books that deal with both subjects, and in a comprehensive manner. The

iii

book is also valuable for its opening chapters that clearly lay out understanding of our creation as tri-part creatures, and for a brilliant apology as to what inner healing actually is, dispelling confusions and errors. Our own book by nearly the same title was also an attempt to say that inner healing and deliverance go together, and in many instances one should not be done without the other. It is a blessing to find another warrior team in Christ buttressing and adding to that teaching. Put the book to work in small group ministry; the contents contain a readymade curriculum dealing with aspects of character that small groups can study week by week, practicing the Scriptures that say to confess our "faults" to one another and "speaking the truth in love."

John and Paula Sandford
Elijah House Ministries and bestselling authors

There is no greater need in the body of Christ than the ministries of deliverance and personal healing. However, because of past misuse and abuse in the name of deliverance, these ministries have sadly been rejected by many denominations and churches. The result has been a less-than-victorious Bride of Christ. The church is full of hurting people who hurt themselves and others.

The authors of this book have done a great service for the body of Christ. They have taken the *weird* out of deliverance and personal healing and have put together one of the most comprehensive, line upon line, scripturally sound and well-balanced books I've ever read on these subjects.

Deliverance and personal healing truly are the children's bread. I highly recommend this book for all believers, but especially for ALL pastors, counselors and deliverance ministers.

Bill Sudduth
Ambassador
International Society of Deliverance Ministers
Colorado Springs, Colorado, USA

Spiritual Warfare A Comprehensive Guide to Personal Healing and Deliverance by Drs. Jerry and Sherill Piscopo will give the believer an extensive understanding about the subject of Deliverance and Inner Healing. I (Sandra) have known and worked under the Piscopos for more than twenty years and have experienced firsthand the revelation and application of the knowledge gained by this powerful Apostolic Team! It is a personal prayer answered to see their years of dedication and commitment to binding up the brokenhearted and setting the captives free brought out of obscurity and put in book form to reach out even more to the Body of Christ. This book can and will take the reader to another level in their relationship with the Lord as they apply the principles contained in this book.

What impressed me (Alonzo) so much about the Piscopos is that they are first partakers of their own ministry by submitting themselves on a yearly basis, allowing them to author a comprehensive guide to *personal* healing and deliverance. This book is of apostolic origin because it can be utilized, as stated in Ephesians 4:12a, to perfect and equip the saints for the work of the ministry. The book provides a model for deliverance and inner healing that can be established in any church or ministry by anyone who reads and applies the techniques, methods and vast knowledge in this book reflecting over twenty-five years of ministry. I know personally because we have duplicated their monthly seminar in our church for the past several years based on the information contained in this book.

Drs. Alonzo T. Sr. and Sandra R. Gay
Acts Ministries Inc.
Winter Haven, Florida

The Piscopos have written a book that is comprehensive and scriptural. This is the kind of book that all believers need to have in their library both to read and to reference. This will help set not only this present generation, but ones to come, free.

Dr. Cindy Jacobs
Generals International and bestselling author

Table of Contents

Foreword

The book you hold in your hands is not only instructional but also prophetic.

Why do I say it is prophetic?

We live in extraordinary times. The Second Apostolic Age began, to the best of my calculations, in 2001, not many years ago. The First Apostolic Age is dated around one hundred or two hundred years after Jesus and His apostles. In other words, for some 1,800 years the church lacked true biblical government, namely the foundation of apostles and prophets as we see in Ephesians 2:20. The Holy Spirit began repositioning the Body of Christ around the middle of the twentieth century, and by 2001 a critical mass of the church had moved into the new wineskin with the trend still continuing.

Why is this important? We are now witnessing one of the most radical changes in the way of doing church since at least the Protestant Reformation. A growing number of believers, churches, and ministries are now properly aligned with apostles and prophets; therefore, God is able and willing to entrust His people with powerful areas of ministry for advancing His kingdom that the church was not ready for previously.

Two areas of ministry that God is unfolding in today's church are deliverance and inner healing. That is why I see this book as prophetic. It is pointing the way for the body of Christ in general to embrace the biblical commands that we are to "cast out demons and heal the sick" (physically and emotionally). The same Holy Spirit that anointed Jesus to preach the gospel to the poor, heal the brokenhearted, preach deliverance to the captives, recovering of sight to the blind, to set at liberty them that are bruised, and to preach the acceptable year of the Lord (Luke 4:18-19) is the same Holy Spirit that anoints the Church today. This book, *Spiritual Warfare A Comprehensive Guide to Deliverance and Personal Healing,* is a solid and reliable guide for setting people free from the harassment of evil spirits wherever and whenever they may appear.

Jerry and Sherill Piscopo are part of the small band of courageous leaders who pioneered deliverance ministries as far back as the 1970s.

They did not have much affirmation from other Christians back in those days. Most of the church regarded deliverance and inner healing as strange or scary or flaky or on the lunatic fringe. But the Piscopos were undaunted. They engaged in deliverance and inner healing ministries not to please the public but in obedience to the biblical mandate from Jesus and the apostles. Almost every time Jesus sent out His people to preach the gospel of the kingdom, He told them to "cast out demons and heal the sick" wherever they went. One time the disciples came back to Jesus enthused and excited, saying, "Lord, even the demons are subject to us in Your name" (Luke 10:17).

Even though deliverance and inner healing ministries are now growing among churches in general, few if any maintain the rigorous, intensive, and sustained schedule that we find in Evangel Christian Churches where the Piscopos are based. For more than twenty-five years they have sponsored monthly Spiritual Warfare Seminars. The vast experience that Jerry and Sherill have accumulated is explained clearly, simply and forcefully in this book. It will be used as a reference and guidebook for churches and inner healing and deliverance ministries throughout our nation.

In order to help spread the word about deliverance ministries, Sherill Piscopo became one of the founders of the International Society of Deliverance Ministers (ISDM) in 2003. ISDM is a professional society currently bringing together more than two hundred respected deliverance ministers to connect with each other, learn from each other, and attempt to raise the water level of deliverance ministries across the country. Go to *www.deliveranceministers.org* to find a map of the USA that will lead you to information on recognized deliverance ministers in your area. People in need from all over the world fly to the Piscopos' monthly conference for help, but part of Jerry and Sherill's vision is to replicate what they are doing throughout the nation so that help is available closer to home. That is one reason why they wrote this book.

Yes, *Spiritual Warfare A Comprehensive Guide to Deliverance and Personal Healing* is a prophetic book. It will help open doors for individuals, churches, and ministries to grasp the essentials of inner healing and deliverance so that the power of God can flow freely far and wide. When you read it you will see that you too can be set free from the enemy's strongholds. Then you can become one of those who fulfill Jesus' command to minister freedom to those around you in need.

Not long ago I read this letter: "A few weeks ago I attended the Deliverance Seminar, which changed my life forever. Before I came to Evangel I had no idea of the true meaning of deliverance. My eyes have been opened to a whole new realm of living and living free in Him. I have learned that deliverance is truly the children's bread!"

This book tells how both inner healing and deliverance are mandated and ministered, and you will love it!

C. Peter Wagner
Presiding Apostle, International Coalition of Apostles

Introduction

Jerry and Sherill Piscopo are truly anointed servants of God. It has been my privilege to know them and work with them for nearly twenty years. They are people of faith, vision, and compassion; they have ministered personal healing and deliverance to thousands of hurting and tormented people. It is of note that many ministers have sent their staffs and leaders to the Piscopos' ministry for freedom and healing.

Throughout the years of overseeing their ministry and their work in the ministries of deliverance and personal healing, I have advised them, counseled them, and observed their dedication to God and His Church. The Body of Christ can now benefit from the Piscopos' expansive understanding and experience in their book *Spiritual Warfare A Comprehensive Guide to Personal Healing and Deliverance.*

You will find this book to be an excellent tool to help people out of the valley of despair as demonic and generational curses are broken off. No one person has all the answers or becomes an authority on demonology, but the Piscopos have studied, researched, and practiced what Jesus gave us to do in the Great Commission (not the great suggestion), "Heal the sick and cast out devils" (Mark 16:15-20, KJV).

This book is a necessary read for every pastor and ministry that will follow the Great Commission to preach and practice deliverance and personal healing. Demons are real. They exist to oppress, possess, and destroy lives. God's answer is to preach the Kingdom of God, cast out these evil spirits, and bring healing to the brokenhearted in the name of Jesus, the blood of Jesus, and the power of the Holy Spirit.

If you do what Jesus said to "do," you will get the results He said you would. You will be able to bring wholeness to people who need help in the process of winning the victory over dark spirits that are occupying territory that belongs to God. These evil spirits must be evicted and exposed as the imposters and squatters that they are.

Some people ask, "Can a Christian have a devil?" or "Can a devil have a Christian?" Through testimonies from thousands of people who have found freedom through the ministry of healing and deliverance, the answer is a resounding "Yes!"

Study this book, and read it carefully and prayerfully. Allow God to shape you into His instrument in order to be His hand extended to a hurting world.

Thank you, Jerry and Sherill Piscopo, for a timely and much-needed resource.

Dr. Emanuele Cannistraci
Founder, Apostolic Missions International, San Jose, CA

Preface

This book is the culmination of more than twenty-five years of experience that my wife, Dr. Sherill Piscopo, and I, Dr. Jerry Piscopo, have gained in areas of inner healing and deliverance. As Christians, we received ministry in several inner healing and deliverance sessions, setting us free from bondages, yokes, and strongholds that could not have otherwise been broken. Soon after, God brought others to us who were seeking freedom. In the years following, we intensely studied Scripture to learn the biblical foundations and principles of inner healing and deliverance. We then taught these to others to help them operate in these ministries. For more than twenty years we have conducted monthly inner healing and deliverance seminars, and have seen thousands of people receive revelation and understanding that has led to their freedom from demonic contamination and emotional pain and bondage. We have included selected anonymous quotes from testimonies sent to us from people throughout the world. We also receive yearly ministry in these areas ourselves as part of our sanctifying process; it is important that we remain committed to what we believe in.

The book contains our personal experiences, teachings, and practical lessons learned through ministering to others. We have endeavored to give guidance and instruction in an easy-to-read format. Our desire is to share the wisdom, insights, and revelations God has given us so that you may be well-equipped to help others gain freedom. We write with a spirit of humility and honesty. We do not pretend to know everything in these areas, and many have gone before us from whom we have learned much. However, no two ministries are alike, and inner healing and deliverance ministers approach their roles from different perspectives.

Our bodies have two hands that look alike and perform similar functions, yet they still have individual roles to fulfill and duties to perform. The same is true for those who administer inner healing and deliverance. God distributes his gifts as he sees fit (1 Corinthians 12:11), but there are different administrations of the same gift. We commend those who labor in these areas and exhort them to continue in the ways God has shown them so that he may receive the glory. God continues to reveal new truths and insights to his children, and he has given my wife and me unique perspectives on inner healing and deliverance. The Bible says we "know in part" and we "see in a mirror, dimly" (1 Corinthians 13:12). Only Jesus has a complete perspective on setting his children free.

We hope this book either gives you your first insight into the ministries of inner healing and deliverance or adds greater revelation and understanding to what you have already received from the Lord.

Jesus spoke publicly in a synagogue for the first time in Luke 4:18-19. He quoted Isaiah: "The Spirit of the Lord GOD is upon me; because the LORD hath anointed me to preach good tidings unto the meek; he hath sent me to bind up the brokenhearted, to proclaim liberty to the captives, and the opening of the prison to them that are bound;

to proclaim the acceptable year of the LORD, and the day of vengeance of our God; to comfort all that mourn;" (Isaiah 61:1-2).

These verses are the biblical foundation for inner healing and deliverance, and are significant for several reasons:

- Jesus tied Old Testament prophecy to New Testament revelation.
- In preaching the Good News to the poor, he stated he was the Messiah.
- As the Messiah, he had come to set his people (prisoners) free from the works of the law. He also *delivered* them from demonic bondages and strongholds the enemy had held them in, as recorded in the New Testament.
- In recovering sight for the blind and releasing the oppressed, Jesus did more than heal those who were physically blind; he also ministered to the hurts and wounds of their souls, which opened their spiritual eyes to the oppression they were under. This is *inner healing* (some may call it soul healing, binding up the brokenhearted, or similar names).
- The year of the Lord's favor not only applied to people in Jesus' time but continues today. In keeping within the context of the above-mentioned Scripture, his favor relates to defeating the enemy while offering deliverance and inner healing to all who come to him.

As we continue to study God's Word, Dr. Sherill and I find references to inner healing and deliverance on almost every page of the Bible. Why? Because these two ministries are part of God's redemptive plan for his children. Please note that we said these are for *his children* and not necessarily for the unsaved as many believe. God redeemed us from the enemy in *all* areas of life through his finished work on the cross. He is our Redeemer, our Deliverer, and our Healer. Jesus is the greatest love of our lives. Seeing souls saved and seeing Christians set free are the greatest desires my wife and I have.

Our book presents a comprehensive look at inner healing and deliverance. Line upon line and precept upon precept, we show that inner healing and deliverance are found throughout the Bible. You will discover the authority you have as a believer over Satan and his demonic hosts. We do not need years of experience to combat the enemy. We need to understand the victory Jesus has gained and the authority he has given us. God desires to set us free in all areas of life so we can effectively minister inner healing and deliverance to others.

May God richly bless you.

—Drs. Jerry & Sherill Piscopo
Detroit, Michigan

Dr. Jerry Piscopo's Vision

In 1980, God gave me a vision that became my call into the ministries of inner healing and deliverance. This vision has been foundational to all other ministry endeavors that Dr. Sherill and I have embarked upon. Here is my vision:

I was walking up the side of a hill that I could not see over. A slight breeze blew all around me. The wind symbolized the presence of the Holy Spirit. When I reached the top, I looked across a valley and saw thousands of demons lined up single file on the other side. They were talking and laughing, but noted I was watching them.

I felt overwhelmed as I faced them, but not intimidated. The wind was a reminder of God's omnipotent power. I also knew the demons could not cross the valley separating us.

I looked to my right and saw a woman coming alongside me. Her presence strengthened me and I was ready to do battle, but I did not know how we could defeat so many demons at once. When I later met Dr. Sherill, I knew she was the woman in my vision and would one day be my wife.

When I looked behind me, I saw hundreds of people standing single file just below the ridge-top. Tears filled my eyes as I understood they were brothers and sisters in Christ. In the following days, I realized these people represented many whom Dr. Sherill and I were to train in inner healing and deliverance, while others were seasoned ministers in their own right. They had been set free from the enemy's strongholds and specialized in the areas of inner healing and deliverance. They also knew their authority in Christ over the enemy. These people moved up to the top of the ridge in one unbroken line. When the demons saw them, they froze in fear. We were now ready for battle, with victory assured.

God used this vision to confirm my calling into the ministries of inner healing and deliverance. Over the years it has supernaturally strengthened me, in like fashion to the food given to the prophet Elijah (1 Kings 19:7-9). Whenever I feel battle-fatigued, I take time to dwell on this vision to regain my focus and strength. Every person who is set free from the enemy's grasp is added to the thousands in my vision. The Lord's army is growing on a continual basis. As we battle together against our common enemies, God's Word assures us that victory is ours.

—Dr. Jerry Piscopo

Prologue

I, Dr. Jerry, became a Christian under very unusual circumstances. Prior to my conversion in the 1970s, I grew up in an upper-middle-class home on the east side of Grosse Pointe Woods, Michigan. My parents were Italian immigrants. My father owned an automobile dealership and my mother was a housewife. Although we looked liked the perfect family, there was a dark reality to our environment. My father was a professional gambler, a card and dice cheat, and an alcoholic. He sometimes physically beat my mother while in a drunken stupor. My extended family also had many acquaintances in organized crime.

I attended private schools and graduated from the University of Detroit with a business degree in 1973. I had planned on entering law school, but that same year my parents tragically died within ten days of each other from cancer. I inherited my father's automobile business and decided to take it over instead of attending law school. I thought it would be a very lucrative business.

I met my first wife in high school. We married in 1974, but it lasted only a couple of years. I was too busy drinking, gambling, cheating, and womanizing; she soon tired of my lifestyle. My subsequent divorce in 1977 drove me to my knees, and I accepted Jesus Christ as my Savior in the early part of the year. I suffered tremendous guilt because of my lifestyle; my ex-wife did not deserve such treatment.

I knew I had to change, so I turned to God. I soon started attending 6:00 a.m. mass every morning. One morning while praying, I confessed my need of God and begged forgiveness from Christ. In reply, I heard an audible voice say, "Live a good, clean life, according to my Word."

I looked around to see who was speaking, but the sanctuary was empty. I realized God had spoken to me. But I had no idea what he meant. For the next two years, I attended morning mass and continually read my Bible. I also kept up my gambling, drinking, and carousing; I didn't know how to let these things go.

In 1979, I met Dr. Sherill through her former husband. She was a Christian. When she invited me to a local Bible-believing church, the "Voice" I heard in that empty sanctuary spoke to me again. "This is where I have placed you," he said. I finally understood that God wanted me to live my life according to the Bible.

I was hooked.

I became a regular church attendee, took basic doctrine classes, helped out in various ministries, and developed a strong personal devotional and prayer life. For the next seven years I worked tirelessly at a youth home once a week, became a head usher, was involved in the altar and prayer ministries, taught a Sunday School class, helped in a convalescent home, volunteered to for Salvation Army church services, and hosted radio and television programs. I also made sure I was accountable to the elders at my church and met frequently with them.

By developing a solid Christian foundation through studying my Bible, listening to good teaching, and being water baptized, the Lord slowly took away my worldly desires. The smoking, drinking, and gambling were replaced with a fervency for him. However, there was still a strong spirit of lust operating in my life. I could not break the bondage of womanizing. I cried out to God to set me free. Soon after, he used a prophetess to deliver me from this vice. Then he used her to launch me into the ministries of inner healing and deliverance. Here is the sequence of events that transpired:

While walking to the bank in 1977, I glanced down and saw a tract. It was from the ministry of Roselyn Musselman, an evangelist and prophetess, who had a national radio broadcast dealing with inner healing and deliverance. I was intrigued by the tract and called to order some. She agreed to send them, then asked, "Would you mind if we met so that I could pray for you?"

I met Roselyn at her home along with two intercessors who served with her. As soon as I sat down, they began their warfare prayers. Roselyn prayed over me for what seemed like hours, and dealt with a myriad of oppressing spirits and prayed through specific inner healing memories. As each issue was resolved, freedom and peace replaced the torment. When my session ended I felt completely free, especially from the sexual oppression. In the days following, God's presence filled my spirit. I felt his anointing upon me. I have not struggled with any of the areas we dealt with since that time. My own experiences proved the power of inner healing and deliverance to me, and God used them to birth my own ministry.

In early 1985, Dr. Sherill went through a heartbreaking divorce after finding out her husband had been having affairs for years. We had remained friends for several years, and I knew God wanted to heal her from past hurts. I had formed an inner healing and deliverance team, and we prayed for several hours over Dr. Sherill. God was faithful over time to heal her from the repercussions of an alcoholic family life, deliver her from the bondage of bulimia (with an addiction to laxatives), and set her free from performance-driven desires for approval. We married in the spring of 1986, and she joined me in full-time ministry after leaving her job as a high school teacher.

Over the past twenty-five years, Dr. Sherill and I have gained a great deal of knowledge, insight, wisdom, and revelation in areas of inner healing and deliverance. We want to pass along our knowledge to both professional and lay ministers who want to see others set free. These ministries are part of our covenant with God. Deliverance is the children's bread (Matthew 15:21-28), and Jesus ministered inner healing to the woman at the well (John 4:4-28). The same Holy Spirit who anointed Jesus in Luke 4:18-19 also wants to anoint men and women today to set people free. It is our prayer that God uses this book to teach you the truths of inner healing and deliverance and how to effectively work in these ministries.

CHAPTER 1

A Triune Being

Man is a triune being, consisting of spirit, soul, and body. Satan desires to prevent us from being born again (spirit); he works to infiltrate our minds, memories, wills, and emotions (soul); and he tries to bring sickness, disease, and infirmity upon us (body).

It is easy to distinguish between one's body and soul. John wrote that he desires us to prosper and be in good health (our body) even as our souls prosper.[1] However, it is more difficult to distinguish between the spirit and soul.

"For the word of God is quick, and powerful, and sharper than any two-edged sword, piercing even to the dividing asunder of soul and spirit, and of the joints and marrow, and is a discerner of the thoughts and intents of the heart."[2]

The Bible clearly differentiates between spirit, soul, and body. Let's take a look at man as a triune being.

Testimony

"I'm able to recognize the voice of God like never before, and can actually detect the enemy at work now and head it off. I have begun to do warfare."

1

The Spirit

When we become what the Bible calls "born again," there is a rebirth of our human spirits.[3] We become alive in Christ, and we can commune with God as Adam did in the Garden of Eden. We reach out to God with our spirits, and through our spirits we come to know him. God is a Spirit, who took on a man's body through his son, Jesus Christ.[4] Doing so did not make him any less God. The real man is not an outward man, but the inward man, the unseen spirit man. Paul emphasized that the spirit is the very heart of a man.[5]

It is important to understand that each of us has a spirit, otherwise we can easily confuse thoughts and feelings emanating from our souls with the work of our spirits. This does not mean God can't direct us through our souls. However, our spirits are the primary means of communion with God. Here are some scriptural references:
- "He that hath no rule over his own spirit is like a city that is broken down, and without walls" (Proverbs 25:28).
- Zechariah 12:1 tells us that it is the Lord who forms the spirit of a man.
- "For what man knoweth the things of a man, save the spirit of man which is in him? even so the things of God knoweth no man, but the Spirit of God" (1 Corinthians 2:11).
- 1 Corinthians 5:4-5 speaks of man's spirit twice.

"God is a Spirit: and they that worship him must worship him in spirit and in truth" (John 4:24). Our spirit has three main functions: conscience, intuition, and communion.

Conscience

Our conscience discerns the difference between right and wrong, based not on knowledge or experience but on confirmation or conviction by the Holy Spirit. Often, we reason away what our consciences judge. The Holy Spirit judges by the Word of God; he doesn't consider worldly opinions when he confirms or convicts us in our consciences. If we are doing something wrong, our spirits will raise their voices in conviction. If we are doing what is right, our consciences will be at peace. The Bible mentions actions that occur in our spirits:

- "But Sihon king of Heshbon would not let us pass by him: for the LORD thy God hardened his spirit, and made his heart obstinate, that he might deliver him into thy hand, as appeareth this day" (Deuteronomy 2:30).
- "Create in me a clean heart, O God; and renew a right spirit within me" (Psalm 51:10).
- "When Jesus had thus said, he was troubled in spirit, and testified, and said, Verily, verily, I say unto you, that one of you shall betray me" (John 13:21).
- "I had no rest in my spirit, because I found not Titus my brother: but taking my leave of them, I went from thence into Macedonia" (2 Corinthians 2:13).

Paul tells us that by submitting to the Holy Spirit through our consciences, we can express and live a righteous life, a spirit-led life. Through our consciences, the Holy Spirit empowers us to have right motives, think right thoughts, speak right words, and do right deeds.[6]

Righteousness is holiness in character and conduct. It is letting Jesus live through us. When people see righteousness produced in our consciences through our lives, they will glorify God.[7]

Our conscience forewarns us of thoughts or actions that are not pleasing to God. Even while we are considering a particular thought or action, our consciences immediately let us know whether or not God approves—as long as we are in tune with our spirits. It also convicts or commends us long after our words have been spoken or actions taken.

> *Righteousness is holiness in character and conduct.*

Testimony

"My marriage is so much better! I am warring with the scriptures and praising God."

3

Intuition

Intuition is the spiritual counterpart to our souls' feelings and senses.

It is through our intuition that we "sense" something independent of any outside influences and interactions with the spirit world. It is the place of discernment and the place where the "gift of discerning of spirits" resides.[8] Our intuition lets us *know* something, while our minds help us to *understand*. God gives revelation, teaching, and guidance to us in our intuition.

The Bible teaches us that our spirits
- are willing;[9]
- can perceive;[10]
- are moved and troubled;[11]
- can be stirred;[12]
- can know our thoughts;[13]
- can bless.[14]

Our spirits also "feel" things in the spiritual realm. The Bible records that Jesus *sighed* in his spirit.[15] Jesus said we can *worship* the Father in spirit and truth.[16] Paul tells us to be fervent in spirit.[17] Our spirits can sing and bless.[18] We can also love in our spirits.[19] These are just a few of the "feelings" in our spirits.

> *Our intuition lets us know something, while our mind helps us to understand.*

Like the conscience, intuition does not need any outside influences to direct it. The impact of our consciences comes without reason, and in a straightforward manner. It warns us, constrains us, exhorts us, agrees or disagrees with us, and commends us without consulting our bodies, our souls, or the world around us.

Communion

In order to commune with God, we must possess a similar nature.[20] It is through our spirits that we are able to commune with him. The Holy Spirit searches all things, including the deep things of God, then he reveals them to us.[21] As with the conscience and intuition, our spirits' communion with God is direct.

In our communion with him, the Holy Spirit will teach and guide us according to the perfect will of God for our lives.

"Howbeit when he, the Spirit of truth, is come, he will guide you into all truth: for he shall not speak of himself; but whatsoever he shall hear, that shall he speak: and he will shew you things to come" (John 16:13).

As we receive instruction in our spirits, God also gives us the ability to impart to others.

The highest form of communion with God comes through worshipping him in spirit and truth. In spirit, we worship him with reverence and humility. He is the King of kings and the Lord of lords. Jesus as God's Word is truth.[22] Communing with God means we are led by the Spirit of God and live according to his Word. When we worship in spirit and in truth, we glorify God.

> *The Highest form of communion with God comes through worshipping him in spirit and truth.*

"For ye are bought with a price: therefore glorify God in your body, and in your spirit, which are God's" (1 Corinthians 6:20).

Communion through worship greatly reverences God; our spirits speak truthfully about his attributes and character. Spiritual worship is our reasonable sacrifice offered to a holy God.

Testimony

"My prayer life is great now. When the attacks from the enemy come, I am able to stand firm against them. I also had a lump in the side of my throat that the doctors cannot explain—it's totally gone!"

The Soul

Our souls are the centers of our personalities. Our souls are the place of our self-consciousness where our minds, wills, and emotions dwell. Intelligence, thoughts, decisions, reasoning, and feelings emanate from our souls. God wants us to line up our thoughts (renew our minds) so we think like he does. Our minds become renewed by studying and meditating on the Word of God—it is our bread of life.[23] The soul realm involves our minds, memories, wills, and emotions—our reasoning, thoughts, and feelings—and is considered part of "our flesh."

The Bible sometimes refers to man as a *soul*.

"And the LORD God formed man of the dust of the ground, and breathed into his nostrils the breath of life; and man became a *living soul*" (Genesis 2:7, italics added).

"Behold, all souls are mine; as the soul of the father, so also the soul of the son is mine: the soul that sinneth, it shall die" (Ezekiel 18:4).

The Mind

Our minds are the centers of our reasoning and thoughts. Our minds are the seats of our intellects, and they allow us to look upon others, circumstances, situations, and ourselves *objectively*. The Bible recognizes the mind of man:

- "And he communed with them, saying, If it be your mind [your decision] that I should bury my dead out of my sight; hear me, and intreat for me to Ephron the son of Zohar" (Genesis 23:8, brackets added). "And Moses said, Hereby ye shall know that the LORD hath sent me to do all these works; for I have not done them of mine own mind" (Numbers 16:28).
- "And they come to Jesus, and see him that was possessed with the devil, and had the legion, sitting, and clothed, and in his right mind: and they were afraid" (Mark 5:15).
- "And even as they did not like to retain God in their knowledge, God gave them over to a reprobate mind, to do those things which are not convenient" (Romans 1:28).

Too often, we are defeated because we listen to the wrong voice—that of our unregenerate minds—or the devil whispering lies.

Our Will

Our wills give us the power to choose. Our wills express agreement or disagreement. Words such as *I will* or *I won't*, *I can* or *I can't*, *I am* or *I am not* represent sentiments of our wills.

The Bible often interchanges the words *will* and *heart*. Scripture is clear: The battleground for our souls is fought in our minds, but our wills are the ultimate prize. We choose whom we serve—self, God, or Satan—through decisions of our wills.[24]

Scripture verses stating the importance of our wills include the following:

- "Come, let us make our father drink wine, and we will [choose to] lie with him, that we may preserve seed of our father" (Genesis 19:32, brackets added);
- "Deliver me not over unto the will [the decisions of] of mine enemies: for false witnesses are risen up against me, and such as breathe out cruelty" (Psalms 27:12, brackets added);
- "Jesus said unto him, 'Thou shalt love the Lord thy God with all thy heart [your will; literally choose to], and with all thy soul, and with all thy mind'" (Matthew 22:37, brackets added);
- "But Peter said, Ananias, why hath Satan filled thine heart to lie to the Holy Ghost, and to keep back part of the price of the land?" (Acts 5:3);
- "For with the heart [act of will] man believeth unto righteousness; and with the mouth confession is made unto salvation" (Romans 10:10, brackets added).

Our Emotions

For many of us, emotions are the most important part of our soul realms. Emotions influence thoughts, views, and opinions. Through our emotions we see the world, others, and ourselves in a *subjective* manner.

They often dictate a person's will. It's like the old saying: "If it feels good, do it."

To be sure, emotions are important. Without them, we would not be able to express ourselves. It is healthy to show both negative and positive emotions, as long as we are in control of them.

A study on the countless emotions the soul can express is beyond the scope of this book. Here are a few scriptures that reflect emotions:

Affection—1 Samuel 18:1; Song of Songs 1:7

Desire—Psalm 84:2; Matthew 12:18

Happiness—Psalm 137:8; Proverbs 16:20

Bitterness—2 Kings 4:27

Sadness—Psalm 42:5, John 12:27

Anger—Genesis 30:2

The soul makes up our *natural* lives. It is the part of our beings enabling us to exist, feel, think, act, and react. It is the real "I," as in "who I am." Before we were born again, we lived strictly out of our souls and bodies. After our born-again experiences, we became new creatures in Christ: old things have passed away and all things have become new.[25] This does not mean that our souls died; it means we no longer have to live according to soulish desires.

It is in the soul that the majority of inner healings and deliverances occur. When our minds come in line with God's truth and our emotions no longer dictate our decisions, our bodies will respond to God's Word. Then we can begin to live out of our spirits, stay in communion with God, and act and do according to his will for our lives.

The Body

When we become born again, our bodies becomes a temple for the Holy Spirit to live in.[26] Because our bodies have desires of their own, we must learn how to bring them into submission and subjection to the leading of the Holy Spirit. They are also part of "our flesh."

"God said, Let us make man in our image, after our likeness: and let them have dominion over the fish of the sea, and over the fowl of the air, and over the cattle, and over all the earth, and over every creeping thing that creepeth upon the earth" (Genesis 1:26-27).

8

"And the LORD God formed man of the dust of the ground, and breathed into his nostrils the breath of life; and man became a living soul" (Genesis 2:7).

In creating mankind from the dust of the earth, God created our bodies to reflect his image and likeness. After Adam and Eve fell, our bodies started to die and became subject to mortal consequences. We know that when we are resurrected we will receive a new body, a spiritual one.[27] In the meantime, we live in a mortal body that is a temple for the Holy Spirit.[28] Let's look at an overview of the body and its functions from a biblical perspective.

Our bodies are important parts of our triune beings. If it were not, God would never have created one for us to live in. We interact with the world around us through our senses—hearing, seeing, tasting, touching, smelling—which are part of our bodies.

When God originally created man, he created us spirit, soul, and body. When Satan tempted Eve to sin, he said, "Ye shall not surely die."[29] After she and Adam ate the fruit from the tree of knowledge of good and evil, their physical bodies began to die and they were spiritually separated from God.

Here is the present condition of our bodies:

"And if Christ be in you, the body is dead because of sin; but the Spirit is life because of righteousness. But if the Spirit of him that raised up Jesus from the dead dwell in you, he that raised up Christ from the dead shall also quicken your mortal bodies by his Spirit that dwelleth in you" (Romans 8:10-11).

The word "quicken" means to *make alive, to give life; to revitalize*. The present condition of our bodies is "dead" because of original sin. It is the Holy Spirit's job (through our own spirits) to bring our bodies back to life. Unlike our spirits, our bodies are not brought back to their original state of perfection. They are still subject to the corruption of this world, to sickness and disease, and to the effects of sin. Until Jesus returns, we will continue to wait for "the redemption of our body."[30]

Even though our bodies are functionally alive, the Bible tells us they are really dead because of the *effects* of sin.

"I beseech you therefore, brethren, by the mercies of God, that ye present your bodies a living sacrifice, holy, acceptable unto God, which is your reasonable service" (Romans 12:1).

Our bodies become *living* sacrifices by receiving life from the Holy Spirit. It is not possible to change the *nature* of our bodies; they are dead. However, when the Holy Spirit gives our bodies life, he actually *strengthens* them to perform the work he has called us to. We also receive the promises of his restoration when we are sick and preservation from sickness when we are well.[31]

As Christians, we experience the futility of trying to control our bodies, our flesh. We crucify our flesh. As Paul says, "For that which I do I allow not: for what I would, that do I not; but what I hate, that do I."[32]

We can only control and dictate to our flesh by yielding ourselves and cooperating with the power of the Holy Spirit. How do we do this? By living according to God's Word and yielding our bodies to be instruments of the Holy Spirit. Only the Holy Spirit can take the finished work of Christ and empower us to live victoriously over the desires of our flesh.[33]

Our Body Is the Lord's

Even as Christians, we allow the desires of our flesh to rule in our lives. For instance, gluttony, immorality, anger, and selfishness are often exhibited by believers.[34] But as temples of the Holy Spirit, our bodies are to be set aside for the Lord.

"Meats for the belly, and the belly for meats: but God shall destroy both it and them. Now the body is not for fornication, but for the Lord; and the Lord for the body" (1 Corinthians 6:13).

Because God is *for* us, he is not *against* us.[35] This means that God is on our side! He does not want us to succumb to the power of sin and to sickness and disease. He wants to deliver us from these. Jesus bore our sins in his body, so that we might die to sins and live for righteousness; by his wounds (stripes) we have been healed.[36]

We are not to neglect our bodies but rather to allow the life of Christ to live through it. We are not to allow its appetites to rule over us. Paul tells us, "But I keep under my body, and bring it into subjection: lest that by any means, when I have preached to others, I myself should be a castaway."[37] Taking care of our bodies, and keeping them disciplined, will equip us for a long life of service to our Lord.

Righteous Living

Our spirits give us life. Our souls give us personality. We live in bodies. Man is a triune being. However, we cannot separate ourselves into three parts. Our spirits, souls, and bodies are distinct, but they also interact with each other. What affects one part affects the others. For instance, it is true medically that a person who harbors anger has a greater risk of having a heart attack. Depression causes an imbalance of body chemicals, and vice versa. When our spirits are attacked, our souls will suffer effects from it. A spirit of rage will send a person into a fitful frenzy. An accusing spirit will cause a person to become defensive. We read that a spirit of murder came upon Saul, who then took up a javelin and hurled it at David, aiming to kill him.[38]

No matter what condition we find ourselves in, Paul's admonition to present our bodies as living sacrifices to God is in contrast to the required Old Testament sacrifices.[39] He tells us this is true worship and involves our spirits, souls, and bodies. By submitting to the power of the Holy Spirit, we can express and live the righteous life God wants us to. The key to living a righteous life is found in the power of the Holy Spirit.[40]

> *Righteousness is holiness in character and conduct.*

The Holy Spirit empowers man as a triune being to have the right motives, think right thoughts, speak right words, and do right deeds. Righteousness is holiness in character and conduct. It is letting Jesus live through us. When we live a Holy Spirit–controlled life, people will see righteousness in our good works and glorify God.[41]

Testimony

"I am battling a lot less with things. I have a tremendous
peace and can stand strong against the enemy;
the oppression is gone."

Chapter 1 Man Is a Triune Being

1 – 3 John 1:2

2 – Hebrews 4:12

3 – John 3:3-7

4 – John 4:24; 1 John 4:2

5 – Romans 2:28,29

6 – Romans 8

7 – Matthew 5:16

8 – 1 Corinthians 12:10

9 – Matthew 26:41

10 – Mark 2:8

11 – John 11:33

12 – Acts 17:16

13 – 1 Corinthians 2;11

14 – 1 Corinthians 14:16

15 – Mark 8:12

16 – John 4:23

17 – Romans 12:11

18 – 1 Corinthians 14:15-16

19 – Colossians 1:8

20 – John 4:24

21 – 1 Corinthians 2:10-12

22 – John 17:17-23

23 – Matthew 4:4

24 – Romans 7:23

25 – 2 Corinthians 5:17

26 – 1 Corinthians 6:19

27 – 1 Corinthians 15:42

28 – 1 Corinthians 6:19

29 – Genesis 3:4

30 – Romans 8:23

31 – Isaiah 53:4-5

32 – Romans 7:15

33 – Romans 8:1-4

34 – Galatians 5:19-21

35 – Romans 8:31

36 – 1 Peter 2:24

37 – 1 Corinthians 9:27

38 – 1 Samuel 18:10

39 – Romans 12:1-2

40 – Romans 8

41 – Matthew 5:16

'

CHAPTER 2

Spiritual Warfare

Throughout our years in ministry, we have heard countless Christians say, "I can't help the way I am." "I can't break free of my past. I can never change." Our experiences teach us that we are bound to our pasts because of hurts and wounds we have incurred. Subconsciously, we equate our present lives to what has occurred in the past and react accordingly. Divorce, emotional and physical abuse, loss, and rejection shackle us to lives of depression, fear, worry, anxiety, and other painful emotions. We feel like helpless victims with no way out.

Our common enemy, Satan, is determined to keep both Christians and non-Christians blinded to his deceptive ways. He wants to fill our minds with thoughts of unforgiveness, bitterness, rage, and anger, and then entice us to medicate our pain through things such as alcohol, illegal or prescription drugs, sex, and pornography. He does not want anyone knowing we can be free from our past through inner healing and deliverance. The good news is that our Lord Jesus Christ came to set us free. He said we could know the truth and the truth would make us free.[1] The word "make" in this Scripture implies a *process:* We

> *Subconsciously, we equate our present life to what has occurred in the past, and react accordingly.*

are not set free from all that binds us in a moment of time. While God is sovereign and fully capable of this kind of transformation, we more commonly walk through processes over time to gain our freedom. We believe God creates opportunity for us to develop intimacy, trust, character, and faith in him during the healing process. Deliverance and inner healing are not quick fixes. Rather, those receiving these must learn how to "walk it out." This involves learning how to maintain freedom.

In referring to the coming Messiah, Isaiah said,

> The Spirit of the Lord GOD is on me; because the LORD hath anointed me to preach good tidings unto the meek; he hath sent me to bind up the brokenhearted, to proclaim liberty to the captives, and the opening of the prison to them that are bound; To proclaim the acceptable year of the LORD, and the day of vengeance of our God; to comfort all that mourn;
>
> Isaiah 61:1-2

Jesus repeated these same words when teaching in a synagogue in Nazareth, then said, "This day is this scripture fulfilled in your ears."[2] Jesus knew that inner healing (he came to bind up the brokenhearted and to comfort all who mourn) and deliverance (he proclaimed freedom for the captives

> *Scripture implies a process: We are not set free from all that binds us in a moment of time.*

and release from darkness for the prisoners) are the keys to setting his children free. The resulting freedom coming through inner healing and deliverance is mentioned in Isaiah:

"To appoint unto them that mourn in Zion, to give unto them beauty for ashes, the oil of joy for mourning, the garment of praise for the spirit of heaviness; that they might be called trees of righteousness, the planting of the LORD, that he might be glorified" (Isaiah 61:3).

Inner healing and deliverance are not gifts given to individual Christians. They are not listed in any of the "gifts" passages of Scripture. Nor do we see a minister of "deliverance and inner healing" listed as one of the fivefold ministries.[3] This is because the entire Body of Christ has been given the mandate for inner healing and deliverance. Jesus passed on his anointing to "them that believe."[4] This explains why there is such a division in the Body of Christ over inner healing and deliverance. Those who believe in this mandate also work in these ministries and testify to their effectiveness.

Inner healing and deliverance are *tools* of sanctification that God has given us to achieve abundant living. However, before we further study these tools, we must understand that we are involved in war against Satan and his demons. This war is called *spiritual warfare*. It rages all around us twenty-four hours a day, seven days a week. Satan started this battle in the Garden of Eden. It will not end until Judgment Day. Whether we believe it or not, every Christian is involved in spiritual warfare. Why? Because we are the Body of Christ and Satan hates us. It is through us that God accomplishes his kingdom work on the earth, including rescuing the souls of those who are trapped in the enemy's camp.

Understanding Spiritual Warfare

It is important to have a clear understanding of spiritual warfare because it can mean different things to different people, depending on denominational views and personal beliefs. Spiritual warfare is the act of engaging the enemy through authoritative and militant prayer, in which we use the blood of Jesus and the Word of God to overcome his tactics. The term itself is not found in Scripture, but the concept is taught.

> *It is through us that God accomplishes his kingdom work on the earth, including rescuing the souls of those who are trapped in the enemy's camp.*

Spiritual warfare is a threefold battle:

- It is a spiritual battle that Satan and his demons wage against the followers of Jesus Christ.
- It is a spiritual battle that a Christian wages against the enemy through warfare prayer.

17

- It is also a battle between God's angelic ranks and Satan's demon powers.

Testimony

"It's so much easier to get into the Word and to hear God's voice now."

Warfare Reality

The war we wage against the enemy is fought in the spiritual realm. However, victory will be evident in the natural realm through physical and/or emotional healing, or a positive change in circumstances. Satan lusts over control and power in this world; he wants to control everyone and everything in it. We see this in his temptation of Jesus:

Then was Jesus led up of the Spirit into the wilderness to be tempted of the devil. And when he had fasted forty days and forty nights, he was afterward an hungered. And when the tempter came to him, he said, If thou be the Son of God, command that these stones be made bread. But he answered and said, It is written, Man shall not live by bread alone, but by every word that proceedeth out of the mouth of God. Then the devil taketh him up into the holy city, and setteth him on a pinnacle of the temple, And saith unto him, If thou be the Son of God, cast thyself down: for it is written, He shall give his angels charge concerning thee: and in their hands they shall bear thee up, lest at any time thou dash thy foot against a stone. Jesus said unto him, It is written again, Thou shalt not tempt the Lord thy God. Again, the devil taketh him up into an exceeding high mountain, and sheweth him all the kingdoms of the world, and the glory of them; And saith unto him, All these things will I give thee, if thou wilt fall down and worship me. Then saith Jesus unto him, Get thee hence, Satan: for it is written, Thou shalt worship the

Lord thy God, and him only shalt thou serve. Then the devil leaveth him, and, behold, angels came and ministered unto him.

Matthew 4:1-11

Satan tempted Jesus to sin by enticing him to use supernatural power for his own needs, to use his power to win over the multitudes, and to compromise with Satan. These temptations are called the lust of the eyes, the lust of the flesh, and the pride of life.[5] Satan not only lost this battle, but he also lost the ultimate war when Jesus arose from the grave. However, he is still trying to capture as many souls as he can, as well as to destroy our lives and testimony here on earth. When Satan succeeds, God hurts—just like a parent does over losing a child.

Because our enemy is spiritual, the weapons of our warfare are spiritual as well.

"For though we walk in the flesh, we do not war after the flesh: (For the weapons of our warfare are not carnal, but mighty through God to the pulling down of strong holds)" (2 Corinthians 10:3-4).

In spiritual warfare, we fight to defend such things as our minds, wills, and emotions; our physical lives, our families and ministries; our cities and country; and the nations of the world.

The Enemy's Tactics

Satan's attack against Christians is threefold. His most powerful tactic is to convince Christians that he and his demons do not exist. Sadly, many Christians do not believe in spiritual warfare. They either do not believe there is an actual battle going on or they do not like the idea of being involved in war. But from Genesis to Revelation, the Scriptures are full of warfare language. We serve a God of war. Two of God's names make direct reference to this: *El Shaddai* and *Jehovah-Tsebaoth*. El Shaddai means "The Strong One, who gives nourishment and provision for his children."[6] Jehovah-Tsebaoth means "The Lord of Hosts" with special reference to warfare.[7]

Those who are going through personal struggles inevitably use warfare terminology. It captures the essence of their thoughts and feelings like no other wording. It is not uncommon to hear a Christian say, "Boy, am I under attack." or "I am in the heat of the battle right now." or even "The enemy sure is hot on my trail this week." Sadly, many Christians have become passive and fearful because of their ongoing personal battles. With no victory in sight, they feel like giving up. Some are satisfied just to accept their salvation, attend church regularly, and participate in a few church-related activities. However, Jesus called us to a different lifestyle. He wants us to develop a deeper walk with him so that we can overcome the enemy's strongholds and vices in our lives.

Satan's second most powerful tactic is to convince believers that we have no authority or power over him.

"Be sober, be vigilant; because your adversary the devil, as a roaring lion, walketh about, seeking whom he may devour" (1 Peter 5:8).

God wants us to remain steadfast in our faith, submit to him, and resist the devil; then the devil will flee from us.[8] The key to overcoming the enemy is submission to God. When we submit to his ways, his Word, and his Spirit, the enemy sees the power of God working in and through us. Without submission, we have limited effective authority.

Lucifer's third most powerful tactic is to deceive us into believing there is no need for spiritual warfare. He was completely defeated on the cross by our Lord and Savior Jesus Christ. He will willingly admit this to believers if it means he can continue to wage war on this earth without being engaged by Christians. Remember, the ultimate prize for both God's kingdom and Satan's is the souls of people. We need to understand that our common enemy continues to capture souls at an alarming rate without them even knowing they are captive to his will and ultimately bound for his kingdom.

Jesus sent out the "apostles" and the "seventy" to teach and preach about the kingdom of God, with full authority over the enemy.[9] He said they were to heal the sick and set the captives free. When Jesus commissioned the disciples, he was also commissioning us—those who believe.

Spiritual warfare must be proactive in order to thwart the enemy's plans. While all prayer can be considered warfare by nature, spiritual warfare prayer is militant and specifically targeted. We actively resist Satan and his demons when they harass others or ourselves, or when we directly engage the enemy to set free those who are in spiritual bondage.

Testimony

"I can't believe it, but my eating habits are better.
I'm not putting junk in my body anymore;
there is a big change!"

The Battle Rages

Spiritual warfare actively takes place on three levels:

Satan and His Demons Versus Christians

The enemy's hierarchy is clearly described in the New Testament:

Finally, my brethren, be strong in the Lord, and in the power
of his might. Put on the whole armor of God, that ye may be
able to stand against the wiles of the devil. For we wrestle not
against flesh and blood, but against principalities, against powers, against the rulers of the darkness of this world, against spiritual wickedness in high places.

Ephesians 6:10-12

Satan's army is highly organized into fallen angels, demons, principalities, powers, and rulers. Let's take a look at his organization.
- Satan: He is a created being, first found in the Garden of Eden.
  He was perfect when God created him, and full of wisdom and
  beauty.[10] He was once in truth, but since his fall he has been full
  of pride, which is self-deception.[11] He despises God and is the
  originator of sin and self-deception.[12] He is a liar and a murderer.[13] In the Bible, he is called the adversary, devil, dragon,
  Beelzebub, prince of this world, Antichrist, accuser of the brethren, and Lucifer. His ambitions include temptation, enticing
  people to sin, deception, accusation, affliction, and opposing
  God and his saints.
- Fallen angels: These are angels who fell with Satan
  from heaven—as many as one-third of all the angels in

heaven—preferring Satan's ways and will over God's.[14] They function as his messengers.[15]

- Demons: They are spirit beings used by Satan to oppress Christians and possess unbelievers, animals, and even inanimate objects. They have both a will and intelligence, and they act according to their evil nature.[16] Their attacks include the following:
    1. Opposing God's people[17]
    2. Hindering God's Word [18]
    3. Holding captives [19]
    4. Blinding the minds of unbelievers [20]
    5. Sowing tares (worldly people) among wheat [21]
    6. Seduction [22]
    7. Troubling [23]
    8. Vexing [24]
    9. Deception [25]
    10. Possession [26]
    11. Tormenting [27]
    12. Buffeting [28]
    13. Resisting [29]

The words "principalities, powers, and rulers of darkness" indicate that Satan's army is set up in military fashion. He has leaders that control legions of demons that attack and/or control individuals, towns, cities, regions, and nations. In 1 Corinthians 2:6-8 there is reference to the "rulers of this age" that caused Christ's crucifixion. It is possible these are high-ranking demonic forces. Scripture also teaches that Satan's hierarchy has a great deal of power, and fights to stop our prayers. This would include territorial spirits, whose existence is supported by the Bible. In Daniel 10 we learn there is a "prince of Persia" and a "prince of Greece" that are territorial spirits working to oppose God's work and defeat the prayers of the saints.

We are aware there is a controversy in the Christian world surrounding whether demons and fallen angels are one and the same. However, we do not feel this point is not worth debating. The truth is we have authority over all of the enemy's kingdom and his demonic cohorts.

Spiritual Warfare

Christians Versus Satan and His Army

In the Old Testament, we read that God had already given the Promised Land to the Israelites.[30] Before they even entered the land, God had given them victory. Their job was to possess it. However, they were to engage their enemies and drive them out as God directed them.[31] In the same way, our Lord Jesus Christ has also given us victory over Satan and his demons through his death and resurrection. But it is up to us to drive out the enemy from our own lives first, then the lives of others through the power of the Holy Spirit. We do this by engaging our enemy in combat through spiritual warfare prayer.

> *It is up to us to drive out the enemy from the lives of others and our own lives through the power of the Holy Spirit.*

For though we walk in the flesh, we do not war after the flesh: (For the weapons of our warfare are not carnal, but mighty through God to the pulling down of strong holds;) Casting down imaginations, and every high thing that exalteth itself against the knowledge of God, and bringing into captivity every thought to the obedience of Christ; And having in a readiness to revenge all disobedience, when your obedience is fulfilled.

2 Corinthians 10:3-6

What are the weapons available to us?

The Word of God, the blood of Jesus, and our testimony; as well as intercession, the communion table, fasting, agreement, holiness, and of course standing firm in our faith.[32]

God's Angelic Hosts Versus Satan's Forces

The Bible states that God's army of angels is called the Host of God, or Heavenly Hosts.[33] In both Hebrew and Greek, the word "angel" is translated as *agent* or *messenger*. Jesus referred to angels many times, and he was also ministered to by them.[34] The book of Hebrews says angels are ministering spirits sent to serve us because we are heirs of salvation.[35] Scripture states

23

there is a hierarchy among angels that includes archangels, principalities, powers, seraphim, cherubim, and also legions of angels.

Archangels: These are the generals in God's army. While Hebrew tradition states there are twelve archangels, one for each Israelite tribe, the Bible names only three: Michael, Gabriel, and Lucifer (Satan).[36] Angels have varying degrees of authority. For example, Michael is called an "archangel" who has command over other angels and is one of the "chief princes" and a prince of Israel.[37]

Other Scripture passages, such as Romans 8:38-39, Ephesians 6:12, and Colossians 1:16 indicate that God created a hierarchy within the angelic world.

Principalities: They are ruling-class angels that are often depicted wearing a crown and carrying a scepter. They are guardian angels over nations and countries, and are involved with the issues and events surrounding these, including politics, military matters, commerce, and trade.[38]

Powers: These angels are ruling monarchs and have higher authority and more power than others.[39] They were created stronger than man, and they are spiritual potentates.

Seraphim: They are among the highest order of angels and serve as the high worshippers of God. They surround his throne singing, "Holy, holy, holy is the Lord of hosts. All the earth is filled with His Glory."[40] Some scholars believe their praise fills the universe and regulates heaven's movement as it emanates from God. Their love and zeal for God burns so brightly that no one, including other angels, can look upon them. Each Seraphim has six wings: two covering its face, two covering its feet, and two that it flies with.

Cherubim: Scholars feel these are beyond the throne of God; they are the guardians of light and of the stars. It is believed that, even though mankind cannot see them, their divine light filters down from heaven and touches everything on the earth. Each Cherubim has four faces: one of a man, one of an ox, one of a lion, and one of an eagle. The ox face is considered the "true face," as in Ezekiel's description of a cherub's face.[41] Cherubim are considered angels ordained for protection. Cherubim guard the Garden of Eden and the throne of God. Some believe they are in the highest class of angels. Cherubim have perfect knowledge of God. They are mentioned in Genesis 3:24, Ezekiel 10:17-20, and 1 Kings 6:23-28.

Angels: They have a twofold ministry and function: worship and service.[42] They have access to both heaven and earth, and have been given charge over the saints of God to protect them.[43] If the Lord were to open our eyes into the spirit realm, we would see countless legions of angels surrounding us for our protection.[44]

Testimony

"I understand my Bible like never before.
My discernment is much keener, and I have real peace."

Three Levels of Spiritual Warfare

Spiritual warfare, or engaging the enemy, also exists on three levels:
1. Ground level: includes deliverance ministry, person-to-person, praying for each other's personal needs, and seeing believers set free from oppressions and bondages in their spirits, souls (minds), and bodies.
2. Occultic level: demonic forces released through activities related to Satanism, witchcraft, "white or black" magical arts, astrology, and other forms of structured occultism.
3. Strategic heavenly level: territorial principalities controlling nations or people groups. Strategic heavenly level warfare prayer is key to taking our cities for God and planting churches.

One of the best examples of the territorial warfare taking place in the heavenlies is recorded in Daniel 10. For three weeks, Daniel had mourned and prayed over a vision he had received from God.

Then said he unto me, Fear not, Daniel: for from the first day that thou didst set thine heart to understand, and to chasten thyself before thy God, thy words were heard, and I am come for thy words. But the prince of the kingdom of Persia withstood me one and twenty days: but, lo, Michael, one of the chief princes, came to help me; and I remained there with the kings of Persia.

Daniel 10:12-13

One of Satan's powerful subordinates came against the prayers of Daniel and also fought against one of God's angels. The Prince of Persia (demonic entity) could not stop, but could hinder, God's answer to prayer. Victory came only after the archangel, Michael, assisted in warfare.

If we try to wage war in territories not assigned to us, we take ourselves outside of the Lord's protection, allowing the enemy to rein havoc resulting in senseless casualties of war.

We want to add a word of caution concerning territorial warfare. This is not an area for those who are inexperienced to enter. We must be called by the Lord and be willing to learn from those who are experienced. Only under God's direction do we enter into battle over specific territories (i.e. cities, states, and nations). In the natural, an army's commander will send troops into targeted areas in keeping with the overall battle plan. If an individual or platoon engages the enemy in territory they are not assigned, needless injuries and deaths follow. The same is true in spiritual warfare. If we try to wage war in territories not assigned to us, we take ourselves outside of the Lord's protection, allowing the enemy to wreak havoc, resulting in senseless casualties of war.

Defeated Christians

Many Christians cannot live consistent and productive lives. In our ministry, we've seen thousands of Christians in bondage because of hurts, oppression, and curses due to various acts of disobedience, the sins of others, or the environment in which they were raised. These devices are used by the enemy to snare people.

26

"The thief cometh not, but for to steal, and to kill, and to destroy: I am come that they might have life, and that they might have it more abundantly" (John 10:10).

The good news is that Jesus has already triumphed over the devil:

> The Spirit of the Lord is upon me, because He hath anointed me to preach the gospel to the poor; he hath sent me to heal the brokenhearted, to preach deliverance to the captives, and recovering of sight to the blind, to set at liberty them that are bruised, to preach the acceptable year of the Lord.
>
> Luke 4:18-19

Jesus has given all believers the same authority he has through the power of the Holy Spirit. In spiritual warfare—and inner healing and deliverance—Christians use God-given authority to heal the brokenhearted and to set at liberty those who are oppressed.

Heal the brokenhearted: Many believers are not living a full and abundant life because of past wounds and hurts. People and circumstances that have wounded us are carried in our memories and continue to affect the decisions we make today. These become chains and fetters binding the saints.

Bring deliverance to the captives: Medical and psychological experts agree that our ancestral inheritances play major roles in determining what our lives will be like. Just as there are physical inheritances, there are also inheritances of sin, and spiritual and environmental attributes. The depth of our captivity will often dictate our responses to the Lord Jesus Christ's desire to set us free.

> *People and circumstances that have wounded us are carried in our memories, and continue to affect the decisions we make. today.*

Set at liberty those who are oppressed:
During our lifetime, we are often involved in practices that give Satan a legal right to oppress us, even after we have become believers in Christ.

Some of these include superstitions, occult practices, and exposing ourselves to ungodly books and movies designed to lead us away from Jesus Christ. We may also come into contact with people who pray against us to their false gods. They can declare curses, bewitchments, enchantments, and hexes that may affect our lives.

These common snares are designed by the enemy to entrap Christians and place us in bondage so we cannot live Holy Spirit–empowered lives. Our salvation is not in question, but our ability to experience the abundant life is severely handicapped. Those who have been trained in spiritual warfare can identify the causes of bondage (through the Holy Spirit's discernment) and assist in setting in motion the deliverance and inner healing God desires to defeat the demonic forces operating in our lives.

Satan's Planned Attack

In his planned attack against Christians, Satan and his demons have three main goals:

1. He wants to prevent people from obtaining salvation by accepting Jesus as their Lord and Savior. Satan hates mankind, because we were created in God's image.[45] In the Garden of Eden, God breathed his breath of life, the Holy Spirit, into us. After the fall of Adam and Eve, mankind died spiritually.[46] Since then, Satan, the prince of this world, has been determined to stop individuals from becoming born again and displaying the life of God.

2. If Satan cannot stop us from accepting Christ, he will attempt to keep us from serving in ministry and maturing as Christians.

3. He wants to entice believers to turn away from God, deny Jesus, and go back to serving "self, the flesh"—thereby destroying themselves. Remember, the enemy only *deceives* us into believing that he is on our side. Once he exploits us for his purposes, he will attempt to destroy us. He is interested only in "using" people.

God's Battle Plan

Even though spiritual warfare involves engaging the enemy, it is important to stress having a proper balance in our Christian walk. As

Christians, our focus must be on God. We chase after him. We give God the majority of our time and energy, and we study his Word and his character. When we know God's truth, we will also know what is *not* truthful. He wants us to study the "real thing" in order to expose the counterfeit.

It is God who gives us discernment, wisdom, and warfare strategies when fighting the enemy. He is a God of restoration! He takes great delight in seeing people set free from the enemy's camp. Satan's plans and tactics have *never* caught God off-guard, and he takes great delight in seeing people set free from the enemy's grip. It is God who gives us discernment, wisdom, and warfare strategies when fighting the enemy.

Here is a battle plan to follow in order to gain victory over the devil's strategies:

1. Resist the devil: As we submit to God we can resist the devil and he will flee. We are not to give the devil a foothold, but to resist him by standing firm in our faith.[47]

2. Stand against the devil: Paul tells us to put on the whole armor of God so we can withstand the devil's schemes. After we have withstood the evil day (of Satan's attack), we are to continue standing (in our faith in God's Word and his power) by remaining dressed in our spiritual armor.[48]

3. Bind and cast out the devil: Jesus tells his disciples they cannot plunder the strong man's house (the devil) until they first bind him.[49] The same rule applies to us today. Those who believe will cast out demons in the name of Jesus.[50] It is interesting to note that Jesus is addressing *believers* who are willing to believe!

Spiritual warfare is a body ministry; it need not be something frightening. God is looking for willing vessels, not just those who feel "qualified" because of their educational backgrounds. We are all called to fight against the enemy. The Body of Christ needs to take a fresh perspective and understand that we have a real enemy who is out to "kill, steal, and destroy." However, at the end of the Bible we see that we are indeed victorious! God wants us to fight the "good fight of faith" in spiritual warfare, because he has already won the war.

Chapter 2 Spiritual Warfare

1 – John 8:32
2 – Luke 4:21
3 – 1 Corinthians 12:28
4 – Mark 16: 15-18
5 – 1 John 2:16
6 – Genesis 17:1-2;
 Genesis 28:3
7 – 1 Samuel 1:3;
 Jeremiah 11:20
8 – James 4:7
9 – Luke 9:1-2;
 Luke 10
10 – Ezekiel 28:13-16
11 – Ezekiel 28:17;
 1 Timothy 3:6
12 – Isaiah 14:13-15;
 1 John 3:8
13 – John 8:44
14 – Jude 6:
 Revelation 12:4
15 – Psalm 78:49;
 Revelation 12:7-9
16 – Matthew 8:29-31;
 Luke 4:35, 41;
 James 2:19
17 – Matthew 13:19;
 2 Corinthians 4:4
18 – 1 Thessalonians 2:18
19 – 2 Timothy 2:26;
 1 Timothy 3:7
20 – 2 Corinthians 4:4
21 – Matthew 13:37-43
22 – 1 Timothy 4:1;
 Mark 13:22
23 – 1 Samuel 16:14

24 – Acts 10:38
25 – Revelation 12:9;
 Matthew 24:4,5
26 – Matthew 4:24; 8:16;
 Mark 7:24-30;
 Acts 8:7
27 – Revelation 9:1-11
28 – 2 Corinthians 12:7
29 – Zechariah 3:1-3
30 – Joshua 1
31 – Joshua 23
32 – Ephesians 5:11, 13-14
33 – Psalm 33:6;
 Luke 2:13
34 – Mark 8:38, 13:32;
 Matthew 13:41; 4:11
35 – Hebrews 1: 14
36 – Daniel 10:21;
 Jude 9;
 Revelations 12:7-9;
 Daniel 8:16-19;
 Luke 1:19, 26
37 – Revelation 12:7;
 Daniel 10:13, 21
38 – Ephesians 3:10;
 Colossians 1:16
39 – Ephesians 1:21;
 Colossians 1:16
40 – Isaiah 6:3; Rev. 4:8
41 – Ezekiel 10:13-15
42 – Revelation 4:11;
 Hebrews 1:13-14
43 – Psalm 91:11-12;
 Matthew 18:10
44 – 2 Kings 6:15-17

45 – Genesis 1:26
46 – Genesis 3:2-5
47 – James 4:7;
 Ephesians 4:27;
 1 Peter 5:8
48 – Ephesians 6:11-14
49 – Mark 3:23-27
48 – Mark 16:17

CHAPTER 3

The Believer's Authority

Testimony

"The urge to make the fast money and spend it is gone;
I've never been happier in my life.
The best change is the clarity of mind and
peace that comes with it."

The basis for our spiritual authority is a legal one. In order to understand how authority works, we must go back to the Garden of Eden. When God made mankind, both male and female, he created them different from the animals. God gave mankind dominion and rule over all things on the earth. This means that Adam (mankind) had *authority* over everything, including Satan himself.[1]

Man was created in God's image, and God gave man free will as well as dominion or authority. All authority was and is God's, but in the Garden a limited portion of that authority changed hands. God delegated *some* of his authority to man and he has never taken it back.

Adam and Eve had something of tremendous value to Satan; he wanted the authority God had given them. He had no power or authority of his own. He had only lies and deception at his disposal. Satan knew that authority is a legally based reality, so he went to Eve and tempted her.[2] In essence, what he said to her was *Why don't you sign over some of your authority to me?* Satan knew that Adam and Eve could use or misuse their authority.

When he deceived them into disobeying God's command not to eat fruit from the tree of good and evil, Satan was able to usurp their authority. Just as God transferred some of his authority to man, so man passed it on to Satan by his choices. Adam and Eve literally handed over their dominion and authority to Satan. He became prince of this world and the prince of the power of the air.[3] When Jesus came to this earth, he came for "that which was lost."[4] Jesus not only redeemed mankind through his blood, he also restored mankind back to his original place of dominion and authority. This includes the earth and Satan!

Because of Jesus' death, burial, and resurrection, Satan has lost his authority on the earth except in the areas where he can deceive man, just like he did with Adam and Eve. He operates the same way today as he did in the Garden, usurping what God has given us as believers. He can operate only through lies and deception. These entice us to sin, and our sin then gives Satan a legal right to take authority in areas of our lives.

Mankind gave his authority to Satan, and Satan can operate through that which is on this earth and in its atmosphere. He can influence the world only to the degree that people choose to live in disobedience to God.

> *Just as God transferred some of His authority to man, so man passed it on to Satan by his choices.*

The Old Testament states that through covenant—an Old Testament way of giving and receiving authority—the Lord gave the children of Israel the Promised Land. However, they had to fight against their enemies in order to take possession. They had a God-given right to the land; but unless they used their authority in warfare, the enemies of Israel would have remained and enjoyed the Israelites' inheritance.

Jesus' last words to his disciples dealt with delegated authority.[5] As believers in Christ, we have been given full authority over the devil. However, it is not *our* authority that we exercise; it is Christ's authority—Christ in us. Greater is *he* that is in you than he that is in the world.[6]

Jesus said, "All power [authority] is given unto me in heaven and in earth (Matthew 28:18, brackets added).

"Then he called his twelve disciples together, and gave them power and authority over all devils, and to cure diseases. And he sent them to preach the kingdom of God, and to heal the sick" (Luke 9:1-2).

Mark 13:34 tells us that Jesus is like a man who had gone on a faraway journey and left his servants in charge.

Here is an example of the way authority works: A police officer has authority to uphold the law. He is backed by the government he works for. If he were to see a truck full of cement (a powerful vehicle) speeding down the road, he has the authority to pull the vehicle over immediately. The police officer's authority overrules the truck's power. As Christians, we are the "spiritual police" on this earth and we are backed by God's government. Our authority can overrule demonic power on this earth.

"And [God] hath raised us up together, and made us sit together in heavenly places in Christ Jesus" (Ephesians 2:6, brackets added).

"And ye are complete in him, which is the head of all principality and power" (Colossians 2: 10).

"And having spoiled principalities and powers, he made a shew of them openly, triumphing over them in it" (Colossians 2:15).

Unfortunately, many Christians do not believe that Christ's authority is also theirs. Many read the miracles, deliverances, and inner healings Jesus and his disciples performed, as well as the spiritual warfare they engaged in, but say these do not happen today. Others may take the initiative to pray, but when nothing happens they let go of their faith and say, "That's what I thought would happen—nothing."

In our previous example, what would happen if the police officer just watched the speeding truck go by, threw up his hands, and walked away? Anyone watching would be astounded and think he had forgotten his authority. Instead, the officer becomes more aggressive and, if needed, calls for backup. So it is with our authority as believers. We are backed by God's authority; we have legions of angels ready for warfare, and can ask other believers to join us in battle when needed.

Satan and his demons will not give up their territory without a fight. The higher the stakes, the greater the fight will be.

"And from the days of John the Baptist until now the kingdom of heaven suffereth violence, and the violent take it by force" (Matthew 11:12).

Just as the police officer needs to use force at times, so does the believer when it comes to spiritual warfare.

> *We can stand against and overcome the trials and temptations Satan brings our way because we are no longer victims but victors.*

Testimony

"The Lord's voice is so sharp and clear, and when the Holy Spirit speaks I respond."

Seated in Heavenly Places

Most Christians focus on their circumstances and situations, and are moved by their feelings. But these are also the realms that Satan uses against us. We must remember that Satan is a defeated foe. However, he still has at his disposal such weapons as lies, deceptions, and accusations. They are the source of his power. He wants to steal, kill, and destroy. As Christians we must rise above our "flesh" and use our God-given authority to defeat him in battle.

"Even when we were dead in sins, [God] hath quickened us together with Christ, (by grace ye are saved;) And hath raised us up together, and made us sit together in heavenly places in Christ Jesus" (Ephesians 2:5-6, brackets added).

We rule in heavenly realms that are far "above all principality, and power, and might, and dominion, and every name that is named, not only in this world, but also in that which is to come."[7] Because we are *in Christ*, all things are placed under our feet, including Satan and his henchmen!

Romans tells us our destiny is to rule and reign in Christ. The Greek word "reign" literally means to reign as kings.[8] We fight not *for victory* but *from victory*! We can stand against our enemy because victory is already ours.

"Thanks be to God, who gives us the victory through our Lord Jesus Christ" (1 Corinthians 15:57).

We can stand against and overcome the trials and temptations Satan brings our way because we are no longer victims but victors.

"We are more than conquerors through him who loved us" (Romans 8:37).

We can claim God's promise that, "Now thanks be unto God, which always causeth us to triumph in Christ, and maketh manifest the savour of his knowledge by us in every place" (2 Corinthians 2:14).

Testimony

"I have more focus. I am spending more time with God,
and many strongholds have been broken."

Using Our Authority

The Hebrew word for *authority* is "rabah," which means *to increase, to bring in abundance, to enlarge, exceedingly full,* and *to grow up.* The Greek word is "exousia" which means *ability, privilege, force, capacity, competency, delegated influence, liberty, rights,* and *strength.* We can see by these words that when Jesus empowered us—meaning he legally and intentionally gave us power through his commissioning—he gave us his *full* authority.

The tendency for Christians who discover their immense power over the enemy is to become enamored by it. Yes, we are to be bold when dealing with the enemy, and we have full authority over Satan and his demons. But we also need to understand their wiles and schemes of deception, and respect their position. The Bible

> *We often mistakenly confuse our authority with our emotions.*

clearly states "pride goeth before destruction, a haughty spirit before a fall"; and we must remember we have authority over Satan because the Spirit of God lives in us. In Acts 1, Jesus told the disciples to wait until they had been baptized with the Holy Spirit. This same Spirit baptized them with fire and new tongues, and empowered them with boldness.

However, we do not need to be baptized in the Holy Spirit in order to cast out demons. There are some very conservative denominations who do not believe in the baptism of the Holy Spirit, yet their members still cast out devils, because God's Word has already given *all* of us authority over evil spirits. The seventy were sent out on assignment. When they returned, they bragged that even demons bowed to their authority. Yet Jesus said, "Rejoice not, that the spirits are subject unto you; but rather rejoice, because your names are written in heaven."[9] At that point in time, none of the disciples had received the baptism of the Holy Spirit.

We must be careful when dealing with the enemy. Just like a police officer is cautious when approaching someone he has pulled over, we cannot be foolish and brash when fighting against the enemy. Even angels know that it is only God who is sovereign over Satan, and that the devil must bow to the name of Jesus. The archangel, Michael, would not dare to pronounce a judgment against the devil, but instead said, "The Lord rebuke thee."[10]

We must seek God's will in each instance before exercising authority over the enemy in Jesus' name. Sometimes we know God's will because it is revealed in His Word. Other times we need a direct revelation. Unfortunately, we don't always walk in spiritual authority because deep down we doubt it. Why? We often mistakenly confuse our authority with our emotions.

There are some days when we come out of church brimming with confidence. The teaching was great, the worship was wonderful, and we are ready to take on the devil. Two days later, everything is going against us and we wonder if we are still saved! We confuse our authority with our feelings. Emotions and feelings do not equate to authority.

Our spiritual authority is based on the fact that we are *in Christ* and God has given us his Word to defeat the

> *Emotions and feelings do not equate to authority.*

enemy. Spiritual authority is based on faith in Christ, not faith in ourselves. Demons will do everything they can to keep us convinced that we lack authority. If they can make us think authority is a feeling, they can keep us from acting when we don't feel confident. We are no threat to Satan if we are uncertain. We will constantly waver unless we rely on the fact that we have authority because we are in Christ and we have God's Word.

Exercising Our Authority

We must recognize that God has equipped us to overcome Satan's power. Paul said "the weapons of our warfare are not carnal [of a fleshly or earthly nature], but mighty in God for pulling down of strong holds" (2 Corinthians 10:4, brackets added). Scripture *mandates* us to exercise authority:

- The disciples: "Then he called his twelve disciples together, and gave them power and authority over all devils, and to cure diseases. And he sent them to preach the kingdom of God, and to heal the sick. ... And they departed, and went through the towns, preaching the gospel, and healing every where" (Luke 9:1-2,6).
- The seventy: "And he said unto them, I beheld Satan as lightning fall from heaven. Behold, I give unto you power to tread on serpents and scorpions, and over all the power of the enemy: and nothing shall by any means hurt you" (Luke 10:18-19).
- All believers: "Verily I say unto you, Whatsoever ye shall bind on earth shall be bound in heaven: and whatsoever ye shall loose on earth shall be loosed in heaven. Again I say unto you, That if two of you shall agree on earth as touching any thing that they shall ask, it shall be done for them of my Father which is in heaven. For where two or three are gathered together in my name, there am I in the midst of them" (Matthew 18: 18-19).
- All believers: "And these signs shall follow them that believe; In my name shall they cast out devils; they shall speak with new tongues; They shall take up serpents; and if they drink any deadly thing, it shall not hurt them; they shall lay hands on the sick, and they shall recover. So then after the Lord had spoken

unto them, he was received up into heaven, and sat on the right hand of God. And they went forth, and preached every where, the Lord working with them, and confirming the word with signs following" (Mark 16:17-20).

- All believers: "And the God of peace shall bruise Satan under your feet shortly. The grace of our Lord Jesus Christ be with you" (Romans 16:20).
- All believers: "Submit yourselves therefore to God. Resist the devil, and he will flee from you" (James 4:7).
- All believers: "Be sober, be vigilant; because your adversary the devil, as a roaring lion, walketh about, seeking whom he may devour: Whom resist steadfast in the faith, knowing that the same afflictions are accomplished in your brethren that are in the world" (1 Peter 5:8-9).

Testimony

"I received revelation concerning my relationship with
the Father, which brought release from false guilt,
abandonment, and false burdens."

Conditions for Authority

Although we have all authority, there are conditions necessary for us to *exercise* it. First, we must have *faith in God* and believe his Word. We must also have the *faith of God* that we can do what he says. Jesus told Peter that the gates of hell will *never* prevail (or overcome) against the church.[11] Second, we must be in unity of belief and purpose.

"But if I cast out devils by the Spirit of God, then the kingdom of God is come unto you" (Matthew 12:28).

When these two conditions are met, we have the keys to God's kingdom and we can minister in God's power, binding and loosing whatever God has already bound and loosed.[12]

Conditions That Resist Authority

The Bible teaches there are three things that negate our authority—lack of faith, a community of unbelief, and the wiles of Satan.

In all things spiritual, faith is foundational. For instance, a man brought his son to the disciples and asked them to cast out the demon in him. However, they could not. Jesus came to them and said:

O faithless and perverse generation, how long shall I be with you? how long shall I suffer you? bring him hither to me. And Jesus rebuked the devil; and he departed out of him: and the child was cured from that very hour. Then came the disciples to Jesus apart, and said, Why could not we cast him out? And Jesus said unto them, Because of your unbelief: for verily I say unto you, If ye have faith as a grain of mustard seed, ye shall say unto this mountain, Remove hence to yonder place; and it shall remove; and nothing shall be impossible unto you.

Matthew 17:17-20

This applies to us today. Without faith we cannot please God, nor can we defeat the enemy.

A lack of faith is also linked to unbelief. When there is a community of unbelievers gathered together, they can come against our spiritual authority. This happened to Jesus:

> *In all things spiritual, faith is foundational.*

And he went out from thence, and came into his own country; and his disciples follow him. And when the sabbath day was come, he began to teach in the synagogue: and many hearing him were astonished, saying, From whence hath this man these things? and what wisdom is this which is given unto him, that even such mighty works are wrought by his hands? Is not this the carpenter, the son of Mary, the brother of James, and Joses, and of Judah, and Simon? and are not his sisters here with us? And they were offended at him. But Jesus said unto them, A prophet is not without honour, but in his own country, and among his own kin, and in his own house. And he could there do no mighty work, save that he laid his hands upon a few sick folk, and healed them. And he marvelled because of their unbelief. And he went round about the villages, teaching.

Mark 6:1-6

Our personal lives and lifestyles will also affect our spiritual authority.

"But now, after that ye have known God, or rather are known of God, how turn ye again to the weak and beggarly elements, whereunto ye desire again to be in bondage?" (Galatians 4:9).

"Jesus answered them, 'Verily, verily, I say unto you, Whosoever committeth sin is the servant of sin. And the servant abideth not in the house for ever: but the Son abideth ever'" (John 8:34-35).

We must *daily* repent of any sins we have committed, read the Word, and pray at all times if we are to maintain and strengthen our faith. These keep us sensitive to the Holy Spirit, who is the source of our authority.

Finally, we need to be aware that Satan is always looking for ways to buffet our authority.

"Lest Satan should get an advantage of us: for we are not ignorant of his devices" (2 Corinthians 2:11).

Whenever we think we're above temptation, we must remember Satan tempted Jesus.[13] Jesus tells us that Satan, the thief, has only one agenda: to steal, and to kill, and to destroy.

God-Given Authority

Throughout the Bible, God worked through men and women, and his Son and Spirit, to speak his message, guide the nation of Israel, redeem mankind, defeat Satan, and build his church. Scripture is full of instances where God gave men his authority over the elements and specific enemies, and to come against those wanting to defeat God's people:

40

- *Moses*. Moses' life is one of God's revealed authority. Throughout Exodus we see God work through Moses time and time again. For example, in a final act against the Egyptians, Israel's sworn enemy, God brought Moses and the Israelites to the edge of the Red Sea. Just when all looked bleak, God said to Moses, "But lift thou up thy rod, and stretch out thine hand over the sea, and divide it: and the children of Israel shall go on dry ground through the midst of the sea."[14] After the Israelites walked across the seabed on dry ground, God told Moses to stretch out his hand again, and all the Israelites watched in awe as the waters collapsed on the Egyptian army.
- *Elijah*. In 2 Kings 2, Elijah and Elisha are on their last mission together. Elisha knew God would take Elijah home and refused to leave his side. When the two approached the Jordan River, Elijah "took his mantle, and wrapped it together, and smote the waters, and they were divided hither and thither, so that they two went over on dry ground" (verse 8). Then Elisha did the same thing.
- *Elisha*. In 2 Kings 6, Elisha was surrounded by the Syrian army. With nowhere to turn, his servant grew fearful. But Elisha asked God to open his servant's eyes to see the horses and chariots of fire surrounding them. He then asked God to blind the Syrian army, and God granted both of his requests.
- *Paul*. Being filled with the Holy Ghost, Paul pronounced judgment against Elymas the sorcerer:
- "And [Paul] said, O full of all subtilty and all mischief, thou child of the devil, thou enemy of all righteousness, wilt thou not cease to pervert the right ways of the Lord? And now, behold, the hand of the Lord is upon thee, and thou shalt be blind, not seeing the sun for a season. And immediately there fell on him a mist and a darkness; and he went about seeking some to lead him by the hand" (Acts 13:10-11, brackets added).
- *All believers*. Jesus said, "But ye shall receive power, after that the Holy Ghost is come upon you: and ye shall be witnesses unto me both in Jerusalem, and in all Judaea, and in Samaria, and unto the uttermost part of the earth" (Acts 1:8).

- *All believers*: "And he [Jesus] said unto them, Go ye into all the world, and preach the gospel to every creature. ... And these signs shall follow them that believe; In my name shall they cast out devils; they shall speak with new tongues; they shall take up serpents; and if they drink any deadly thing, it shall not hurt them; they shall lay hands on the sick, and they shall recover" (Mark 16:15-18, brackets added).

Clearly, Jesus has promised his authority to those who are his own.

Chapter 3 The Believer's Authority

1 – Genesis 1:26-28
2 – Genesis 3:1-4
3 – John 12:31; 14:30; 16:11; Ephesians 2:2
4 – Luke 19:10
5 – Mark 16
6 – 1 John 4:4
7 – Ephesians 1:21
8 – Romans 5:17
9 – Luke 10:20
10 – Jude 9
11 – Matthew 16:18
12 – Mathew 16:19
13 – Matthew 4:1-11
14 – Exodus 14:16

CHAPTER 4

Personal Inner Healing

Testimony

"I am no longer being afflicted
by debilitating panic attacks."

Personal inner healing is a progressive and sanctifying work of the Holy Spirit. It is sometimes called "healing of memories," "soul healing," or "healing the brokenhearted." As we allow the Holy Spirit to reveal painful memories locked inside our conscious and subconscious minds, he can heal the attached emotional pain. Emotional pain holds us in bondage to our pasts. These traumatic memories may have happened long ago, but they are still active in our lives today because they affect present-day emotions, mindsets, and decisions. We can be successful in life, function within our family units, excel at our jobs, and hold ministry positions but *still* need inner healing. The effects of emotional pain on our lives and the need for inner healing can be paralleled to a farmer's field:

In the spring, a farmer's field seems ready for planting. It looks like he has only to till the soil and plant his seed in the fertile ground. However, the astute farmer knows better. During the winter, rocks are often forced toward the surface. They lie just below the topsoil and can damage the farmer's equipment if they are not removed. The weeds have already seeded the ground and must be sprayed with weed killer. Even after planting his seed, the farmer must continually remove weeds. During growing season, pestilence may come and eat the roots, stems, and leaves of the plants. He must spray against these as well. If he doesn't, the ground will still produce a crop but it will not be as fruitful. Year after year the farmer must continually remove rocks and weeds from his land and be on guard against pestilence in order to produce a bountiful harvest.

You can compare that farmer's fertile field to our minds when we are first born: There may be "rocks" (generational hurts and wounds) in our conscious and subconscious that we do not know about. As we grow, these hurts and wounds surface in our lives. They cause damage to our souls, and the resulting painful memories can cause a broken spirit or a wounded heart. These will always adversely affect us. The circumstances in life (pestilence) can conspire against us to further damage our souls. Other people also can inflict hurts and wounds that produce more painful memories. Further, "weeds" often spring up in the form of self-protection, sinful thoughts, bad habits, and wrong behaviors. These further emotionally debilitate us. Even though we continue to grow and function, we cannot live as effectively as we would like to. The harvest we want to see produced in our lives is not nearly as fruitful. When we seek inner healing, we allow the Holy Spirit to reveal the sources of these debilitating "rocks, weeds, and pestilence" that are locked inside specific memories, in order to bring healing and peace into our lives.[1]

Biblical Inner Healing

Inner healing is an ongoing process that helps us break free of negative thought patterns, feelings, and behaviors that can dominate our lives. Some Christians believe in its biblical mandate, while others believe it has no place in Christianity. Those who are against it state that inner healing techniques and therapies are offshoots of teachings of Sigmund Freud, C.G. Jung, and others. They claim that spirit guides are invoked, hypnosis is used, and memories are created due to a therapist's influence. They feel it is nothing more than sorcery and an attempt to manipulate a person's past, present, or future through "creative visualization." They call inner healing counselors "Christianized psychoanalysts" who use the power of suggestion to solve counselees' problems. These same people claim the Bible teaches that moral choices—rather than past traumas—determine our current dilemmas and are solely our responsibility. There are others in the Body of Christ who believe that, when a person becomes a Christian, he or she is "completely fixed" at conversion. They point to Calvary and state that we have been made whole and do not need further restoration after salvation.

It is true that our moral choices greatly impact our current circumstances and situations. It can also be biblically supported that we are responsible for our actions and attitudes. And yes, Calvary is the *finished* work of Christ. However, it is also an ongoing work in believers' lives, and it is our responsibility to tap into it. For example, the New Testament teaches that sanctification and holiness can be divided into two parts: We have been sanctified by Christ, yet we undergo a continual process of sanctification as we appropriate Christ's work of finished grace in our lives. We have been made holy because of Calvary, but we continue to become holy as we draw closer to Christ.

Jesus made inner healing a part of his mandate and ministry on earth.[2] The following characteristics and outcomes govern true biblical inner healing:

- It focuses on the redemptive work of Jesus Christ as recorded in Scripture.
- It involves a healthy relationship between counselor and counselee. There is no dominance, intrusion, control, or guidance used by either party.
- Memories explored are neither manufactured nor denied but are simply treated as facts—if it *feels* true to the counselee, then the counselor accepts it as such. It is not a counselor's job to decide what are true and false memories.
- After receiving biblically based inner healing, a counselee has a greater ability to hear God's voice and obey his Word.
- There is a greater exhibition of the fruit of the Spirit and the character of Jesus Christ in a counselee's life.
- A counselee's relationships with others improve because the person "just feels normal" and no longer feels controlled by his or her emotions. Peace guides his or her thought life and actions.

"When I was a child, I spake as a child, I understood as a child, I thought as a child: but when I became a man, I put away childish things" (1 Corinthians 13:11).

This verse illustrates the changes in feelings and thought patterns that occur after we have received inner healing. Our thinking and emotions "grow up." We are no longer bound to the whims of childhood emotions and reactions because the pain from childhood events and traumatic experiences has been removed.

Healing the Brokenhearted

The Spirit of the Lord GOD is upon me; because the LORD hath anointed me to preach good tidings unto the meek; he hath sent me to bind up the brokenhearted, to proclaim liberty to the captives, and the opening of the prison to them that are bound; To proclaim the acceptable year of the LORD, and the day of vengeance of our God; to comfort all that mourn; To appoint unto them that mourn in Zion, to give unto them beauty for ashes, the oil of joy for mourning, the garment of praise for the spirit of heaviness; that they might be called trees of righteousness, the planting of the LORD, that he might be glorified.

Isaiah 61:1-3

These verses were written by inspiration from God to his covenant people, the Jewish nation, who were the apple of his eye. They illustrate God's heart, his concern, and his desire to see his children set free from hurts and wounds that hold them back from enjoying the fullness of life.

And there was delivered unto him the book of the prophet Esaias. And when he had opened the book, he found the place where it was written, 'The Spirit of the Lord is upon me, because he hath anointed me to preach the gospel to the poor; he hath sent me to heal the broken-hearted, to preach deliverance to the captives, and recovering of sight to the blind, to set at liberty them that are bruised, To preach the acceptable year of the Lord.' And he closed the book, and he gave it again to the minister, and sat down. And the eyes of all them that

48

were in the synagogue were fastened on him. And he began to say unto them, This day is this scripture fulfilled in your ears.

Luke 4:17-21

Jesus spoke these words while in a synagogue in Nazareth after overcoming Satan's temptations during his time in the wilderness. They once again illustrate that part of Jesus' mandate was/is to *heal the brokenhearted* and *to set at liberty those who are bruised*. This is inner healing. Here are the Greek and Hebrew meanings of key words in the above verses:

- bind and heal are the same: to cure, heal, or make whole
- brokenhearted: to have one's heart crushed by devastating grief, sorrow, or despair
- bruised: to break or crack asunder; a shattering into fragments
- captive: already captured; prisoners that were taken

Jesus was saying that he has come to set us free from our painful pasts.

"The LORD is nigh unto them that are of a broken heart; and saveth [avenge, defend, rescue, and free] such as be of a contrite [crushed] spirit" (Psalm 34:18, brackets added).

Whatever the causes may be, the pains of broken hearts are locked inside our childhood memories and traumatic events. It is the Lord's desire to heal these memories and set the captives free.

Testimony

"I smile again from the inside, not just a fake church smile, but a real Holy Ghost smile."

Rightly Divided

"Confess your faults one to another, and pray one for another, that ye may be healed. The effectual fervent prayer of a righteous man availeth much" (James 5:16).

In this verse, the word "faults" is often translated as "sins." However, the actual Greek word is *paraptoma*, which is translated as "offenses."

We confess our sins to God—but sins are forgiven, not healed. On the other hand, faults or offenses can turn into character weaknesses or defects. During inner healing, we confess our faults by sharing our painful pasts with a trusted friend, pastor, or counselor. The other person can then pray and ask God to heal us of the associated pain.

Jesus and Peter

A painful interaction between Peter and Jesus exemplifies the emotional pain attached to a memory, and Peter's subsequent inner healing.

In John 18, Peter warms himself by a fire of coals while the Jewish leaders question Jesus. Three times Peter is accused of being one of Jesus' disciples, and three times he denies it. After the third time, a rooster crows, fulfilling Jesus' prediction of Peter's denial. The Scripture says that "Peter wept bitterly."[3] The traumatic memories of this event were now locked into his mind. From that day forward, any whiff of fire may have reminded Peter of his denial, and the emotional pain and remorse he felt would flood his mind.

In John 21, Peter and the other disciples had been fishing. Jesus was waiting for them on the shore and said, "Children, have ye any meat?"

When Peter realized it was Jesus, he swam to shore. When he approached Jesus, he smelled a familiar odor—a fire of coals. It should be noted that there are only two places in Scripture that refer to a fire of coals—John 18 and John 21. Given what we know about memories, the pain of denying Jesus would have rushed back to his mind in the same way agonizing memories cause us emotional pain. Jesus knew what Peter was thinking and feeling, and ministered to Peter's painful emotions caused by the previous traumatic events. Jesus asked him to confess his love for him three times in order to bring healing to Peter's memory and erase the effects of his three painful denials.

In the Greek there are three kinds of love—phileo (friendship), eros (sexual), and agape (unconditional). Jesus used two of these. He asked Peter, "Do you *agape* me? Do you *agape* me? Do you

After we receive inner healing, the memory remains, but the painful sting is gone.

phileo me?" Jesus showed Peter the truth: Although he had denied Jesus, Peter had always loved him. This realization brought about forgiveness and restoration in Peter's life. From that day forward, the smell of burning coal would remind him no longer of a painful past but of God's unconditional love. The memory would always remain, but the emotional pain would no longer trouble him. This is a key principle: After we receive inner healing, memories remain but the painful sting once associated with them is gone.

You may wonder why this incident represents inner healing. The key to understanding is that Jesus used the coal-burning fire to trigger Peter's memory. When Peter felt the pain of his denial flooding his mind, Jesus reminded him of their mutual love (as implied by the questions asked). It was Jesus' love—his phileo and agape love—that touched Peter's memories and healed them. Peter denied Jesus three times, and Jesus forgave and affirmed him three times through his love. Peter confirmed this when he wrote that love covers (heals and forgives) a multitude of sins.[5]

The Need for Inner Healing

Inner healing is not just for those who have experienced severe trauma. We have all experienced hurts, wounds, and bruises affecting us on some level. If we were honest with ourselves, we would see depravity in our hearts:

> Ah sinful nation, a people laden with iniquity, a seed of evildoers, children that are corrupters: they have forsaken the LORD, they have provoked the Holy One of Israel unto anger, they are gone away backward. Why should ye be stricken any more? ye will revolt more and more: the whole head is sick, and the whole heart faint. From the sole of the foot even unto the head there is no soundness in it; but wounds, and bruises, and putrifying sores: they have not been closed, neither bound up, neither mollified with ointment.
>
> Isaiah 1:4-6

There is no soundness in my flesh because of thine anger; neither is there any rest in my bones because of my sin. For mine iniquities are gone over mine head: as an heavy burden they are too heavy for me. My wounds stink and are corrupt because of my foolishness. I am troubled; I am bowed down greatly; I go mourning all the day long. For my loins are filled with a loathsome disease: and there is no soundness in my flesh. I am feeble and sore broken: I have roared by reason of the disquietness of my heart. Lord, all my desire is before thee; and my groaning is not hid from thee.

Psalm 38:3-9

Truly, we are a sinful people. And we are a hurting people as well! Locked in our memories are "wounds, bruises, and sores" that have not been "bound up" and need the healing touch of the Holy Spirit.

When we are born again, the blood of Jesus cleanses us, and he takes away our records of sin. We are immediately sanctified and made whole in his sight. Yet we also know that as long as we are on this earth, we will continue to sin and be in need of forgiveness. One reason we may sin is due to our past hurts affecting us in negative ways. Our hurtful memories can affect our behavior until the emotional pain attached to each one is healed.

Have you ever heard someone say, "He needs to grow up" or "She is acting like a child"? To grow up means to become mature and no longer act in childish ways. Inner healing helps us to "grow up" because through it the Holy Spirit can deal with the pains of our pasts and set us free from the things that bind us to "childish behaviors."

The Effects of Inner Healing

Over the years, we have found two characteristics common in many inner healing sessions:

1. In a given situation, we will act out of childish emotions until we are healed from the memories triggering them. We can modify our behavior and, for the most part, control our emotions. However, when the pressure is on, we react in childish ways that are familiar to us. For

example, you may know of someone who has a temper. He or she seems to "blow up" at the drop of a hat.

"It's just the way I am," he or she says. "I just can't control my anger."

Not being able to "get past" a particular behavior may indicate a need for inner healing. (Note: There is no set of criteria that can determine when we need inner healing. It is up to each individual to determine this. However, we can all benefit from it.) A counselor can help a person understand how to *control* his or her anger and *modify* his or her behavior, but a counselor cannot remove the *source* of anger. However, inner healing prayer can reveal painful memories triggering the person's temper and heal its root. What God reveals he also heals.

2. What we *feel* is truth to us. As emotional beings, we are often led by our emotions or dictated to by them. For example, if we feel bad, guilty, or shameful, we conclude that we *are* a bad, guilty, or shameful person. We become our emotions. We identify with them in such a way that we conclude we are what we feel.

The Bible is clear: We are to live not by our emotions but by the fruit of the Spirit and the Word of God.[6] Only the sanctifying work of the Holy Spirit can reveal specific memories needing to be healed in order to set us free. Once the pain attached to these memories is removed, we can choose to react differently—because we are no longer being triggered by past hurts.

When God heals our hurts and wounds, and sets us free from the accompanying pain, he does the following:

> *What God reveals he also heals.*

- "He restoreth my soul: he leadeth me in the paths of righteousness for his name's sake" (Psalm 23:3). With our souls restored (i.e. when our minds are no longer bound to painful memories), we can hear God's voice clearer and follow his plans so that his name can be glorified.
- "I said, LORD, be merciful unto me: heal my soul; for I have sinned against thee" (Psalm 41:4). When we act out according to pain from our pasts, we sin. God promises to heal our souls and free us to act according to the fruit of the Spirit.

53

- "For I will restore health unto thee, and I will heal thee of thy wounds, saith the LORD; because they called thee an Outcast, saying, This is Zion, whom no man seeketh after" (Jeremiah 30:17). We know that our emotions affect our health. Often when we are set free from our painful pasts, diseases such as arthritis and cancer—as well as emotional and mental disorders—are also healed.

- "I will heal their backsliding, I will love them freely: for mine anger is turned away from him" (Hosea 14:4). With our painful memories healed, we can *feel* God's love in our hearts and be less likely to backslide. In addition, we no longer feel as if God is constantly mad at us—a complaint many Christians have.

Inner healing is biblical, and it is relevant to Christians today. If the Body of Christ at large continues to walk in brokenness, it can affect our witness to the unsaved world. To those who argue against it, we point out Matthew 12:33: A tree is known by its fruit. In thirty years of ministry, we have testimonies from hundreds of people set free from painful memories affecting their emotions, attitudes, and actions. When these happen, the truth John wrote about becomes a reality:

"Beloved, I wish above all things that thou mayest prosper and be in health, even as thy *soul* prospereth" (3 John 1:2, italics added).

Testimony

"There has been a tremendous change in my life. I read
the Word with clarity.
I am able to go right into his presence.
My prayer life has become a source of joy and not
something I have to do."

Chapter 4 Personal Inner Healing

1 – Other authors have different analogies, such as rings of a tree or stones in a stream.

2 – Luke 4:18-19

3 – Matthew 26:75; Luke 22:62

4 – John 21:5

5 – 1 Peter 4:8

6 – Galatians 5:19-23; Matthew 4:4

CHAPTER 5

The Wounded Spirit

You may be thinking, *Can my spirit really be wounded*? The answer is a resounding yes! When you are born again, your spirit comes alive to God's voice and direction through the power of the Holy Spirit. Because you are now sensitive to the natural and spiritual realms, your spirit is vulnerable to attacks from these domains as well. As you read through this chapter, ask God to show you any wounds you may have suffered in your spirit. Then ask him for his divine healing.

Describing the Wounded Spirit

The Bible states that our hearts are the source of life. Your heart is the center of your being. Throughout Scripture, the words "heart" and "spirit" are often synonymous; their importance cannot be overstated.

"Keep thy heart with all diligence; for out of it are the issues of life" (Proverbs 4:23). This verse tells us to consider carefully what we allow into our spirits, because it will invariably affect our lives. When your spirit is wounded, it hinders the way you function and can stunt your spiritual growth. Your spirit can become wounded through hurtful words, wrong actions, and the attitudes of others. You can also wound your own spirit in these same ways. As well, circumstances in life can come against you, causing you further hurt. We are all victims of a wounded spirit to some degree. No matter what masks we wear in public, our states of woundedness eventually reveal themselves through the words we speak, through our behavior, through our conduct, or through our treatment of others or ourselves.

A wounded spirit is also known as a broken or crushed spirit. The deeper the wound, the greater its negative effect on our spiritual, emotional, and physical lives.

"The spirit of a man will sustain his infirmity; but a wounded spirit who can bear?" (Proverbs 18:14).

"A merry heart doeth good like a medicine: but a broken spirit drieth the bones" (Proverbs 17:22).

Causes of Wounds

Our spirits can be wounded in various ways:
- Heartbreak can be caused by unfulfilled desires or expectations. It leads to deep *sorrow* or *sadness* that crushes our spirits. "A merry heart maketh a cheerful countenance: but by sorrow of the heart the spirit is broken" (Proverbs 15:13).
- Physical, verbal, and sexual *abuse* always cause significant wounds in our spirits.
- *Hurtful words spoken* by others or by ourselves cause deep wounds in our spirits.
  "A lying tongue hateth those that are afflicted by it; and a flattering mouth worketh ruin" (Proverbs 26:28).
  "A wholesome tongue is a tree of life: but perverseness therein is a breach in the spirit" (Proverbs 15:4).
- *Guilt* can greatly incapacitate us, causing emotional and social damage.[1] It ferments within us, leading to myriad psychological disorders.
- Broken hearts and damaged spirits can *damage our relationships*, as witnessed by the prophet Jeremiah, whose heart was broken by his fellow prophets.[2]
- Accidents, tragedies, and traumatic events can also cause wounded spirits.

Effects of a Wounded Spirit

Wounded spirits can damage our spiritual, emotional, and physical health. The severity of our woundedness is borne through our negative thought and behavior patterns. We lament over spiritual wounds by recalling unfair and unpleasant experiences. We become preoccupied with past memories, giving them power over us. We cannot imagine how a good God would ever allow such awful things to happen to us.

A wounded spirit often originates from childhood. The hurtful seeds sown reap negative effects in adulthood. The following poem illustrates this:

Children Learn What They Live

If children live with criticism,
They learn to condemn.
If children live with hostility,
They learn to fight.
If children live with ridicule,
They learn to be shy.
If children live with shame,
They learn to feel guilty.
If children live with encouragement,
They learn confidence.
If children live with tolerance,
They learn to be patient.
If children live with praise,
They learn to appreciate.
If children live with acceptance,
They learn to love.
If children live with approval,
They learn to like themselves.
If children live with honesty,
They learn truthfulness.
If children live with security,
They learn to have faith in themselves and others.

If children live with friendliness,
They learn the world is a nice place in which to live.[3]

Mental Effects

A wounded spirit can have profound effects on your mental wellbeing, including the following:
- Obsessive-compulsive disorders
- Self-protection and blame shifting
- A critical nature
- Nightmares
- Unforgiveness
- Exaggerated confidence or pessimism

Emotional Effects

A wounded spirit also has direct effects on your emotional health, including the following:
- A fearful, suspicious, or distrustful outlook on life
- An inferiority complex
- Difficulty in giving and receiving approval and love
- Addictions and compulsions
- Oversensitivity
- Extremes in our personalities such as isolation or people-pleasing, protectiveness or permissiveness, becoming workaholics or being afraid to work, and perfectionism or slothfulness

Testimony

"I am much more aware of my thoughts and attitudes
and whether they line up with the Word of God."

The Promise of Healing

Only the power of the Holy Spirit can bring true healing to our wounded spirits. Without God's touch on our lives, we will continue to walk with a "limp" in our souls and spirits even though we are committed Christians and on our way to heaven. The good news is that Jesus Christ came to heal our spiritual wounds.

"The LORD is nigh unto them that are of a broken heart; and saveth such as be of a contrite spirit" (Psalm 34:18).

"He healeth the broken in heart, and bindeth up their wounds" (Psalm 147:3).

Through inner healing and deliverance, Jesus can set us free from the prisons of our woundedness. Healing the wounded spirit is first and foremost the work of the Holy Spirit. It is not our work. It takes humility on our part to acknowledge this. Our flesh cannot heal itself. Counseling, behavior modification, and other such practices are important—but only *after* the Holy Spirit has done his work.

> And I will pray the Father, and he shall give you another Comforter, that he may abide with you for ever; Even the Spirit of truth; whom the world cannot receive, because it seeth him not, neither knoweth him: but ye know him; for he dwelleth with you, and shall be in you. I will not leave you comfortless: I will come to you.
>
> John 14:16-18

The Holy Spirit lives inside us. He is our ever-present help in time of need. Only he can bring truth to our innermost parts and wisdom to our innermost beings through his words.[4]

"The words that I speak unto you, they are spirit, and they are life" (John 6:63b).

However, after receiving God's healing, we still have a fundamental part to play to ensure recovery. Practical steps we should take include:

Fellowship

Just as people can be the sources of our wounds, they can also be sources of healing. We need to seek Christian fellowship—taking time to develop friendships, form prayer partners, and submit to godly leadership.

"Not forsaking the assembling of ourselves together, as the manner of some is; but exhorting one another: and so much the more, as ye see the day approaching" (Hebrews 10:25).

Forgiveness

It is paramount to our spiritual healing that we forgive as we have been forgiven. This includes keeping short accounts and releasing grudges and resentments. Jesus emphasized this in his Sermon on the Mount.[5]

Protection

Wisdom dictates that we guard our spirits from further wounds. However, guarding our spirits differs from self-protection. The latter means we hide behind defensive walls that keep others out and hinder us from developing intimacy in our relationships. Guarding our hearts is akin to setting healthy boundaries—we let the good in and keep the bad out. How do we do this? Proverbs 4 offers a guideline:

- Keep God's Word in our hearts to gain wisdom, understanding, and life (verses 1-6).
- Stay away from those who continually hurt us (verses 14 and 19).
- Refuse to listen to those who speak to us in negative and condemning ways (verse 24).
- Consider what we are doing and why we are doing it, and resist old negative habits and patterns (verses 26-27).

God's Perspective

After receiving God's healing of our spiritual wounds, we can begin to see people and situations from his perspective. We all have wounded spirits to some degree. God is well aware of this. He knows that the sins we commit against each other are often borne of our own woundedness.

God has a unique perspective on our lives. Joseph said, "But as for you, ye thought evil against me; but God meant it unto good."[6] It is important to view people as God does and to see life through his eyes. We cannot know what he knows; but seeing people and life from a biblical perspective helps us understand that God is in control and that he will work all things together for our good because we love him and want to serve him.[7]

Resisting the Enemy

During inner healing and deliverance, the enemy is cast out of our lives and our wounded spirits receive healing. However, the enemy does not give up. He is full of anger and vengeance, and wants to reclaim his territory. Through prayer and discernment, we must learn to recognize his fiery darts, his lies and deceptions, and his outright attacks. How do we do this? We submit ourselves to God and resist the devil, and he will flee.[8]

Resisting means we do not give into devilish wiles but counterattack through the power of the Holy Spirit, casting down all things that come against the knowledge of God.[9] When he tries to remind us of our past wounds, we speak God's healing Word over ourselves. We overcome the enemy's lies by speaking God's truth. We maintain a "readiness in the spirit" by remaining sensitive to the Holy Spirit's voice. He can then warn us of attacks in advance.

Confrontation

We often associate confrontation with negative connotations. This is due to our own individual woundedness and experiences. We fear rejection and being rejected. When offenses come, we may confront in anger or we may consciously bury the offenses and pretend they didn't happen. But Scripture tells us we are to "speak the truth in love."[10] We overcome a problem by acknowledging its reality and handling it in biblical ways. Justifying the problem, making excuses, or blaming the past or other people will hinder resolution. We are to deal with issues, not hold grudges or resentments. Speaking the truth in love includes giving and receiving forgiveness. However truth is revealed, we must be willing to deal with issues in ways that lead to resolutions and restored relationships. God will do his part if we do ours. Relationships may be instantaneously healed or may take time, depending on each situation. Either way, healthy and positive confrontation can lead to healing wounds within our spirits.

The End Result

Healing a wounded spirit is a lifelong process. It will result not in absolute perfection during our lifetimes but in Christlike attitudes and emotional maturity. These lead to our changing from "carnal" believers to "spiritual" believers. Healing our wounded spirits results in transformed minds—and lives! We will think, feel, and act in whole and healthy ways. Transforming our thought lives can lead to balanced emotions and the freedom to control our wills.

Healing our wounded spirits will impact our lives with a spirit of power and love, and sound minds.[7] Our power comes from the Holy Spirit. He enables us to live in love and have healthy mindsets. As we continue to submit our wounded spirits to God's healing power, we will gain love, joy, peace, patience, faithfulness, gentleness, and self-control in ever-increasing measure. Others will see the differences in us. They may even ask, "What has happened to you?" This gives us opportunities to share our testimonies with them—bringing glory to God.

Testimony

"I have less chattering in my mind, a greater appetite
for the things of God, and a greater increase in
praise and worship."

Chapter 5 The Wounded Spirit

1 – Psalm 38:4-10

2 – Jeremiah 23:9

3 – Copyright © 1972/1975 by Dorothy Law Nolte, Ph.D. (This is the author-approved short version.)

4 – Psalm 51:6

5 – Matthew 6:14-15

6 – Genesis 50:20

7 – Deuteronomy 10:12-13; Romans 8:28

8 – James 4:7

9 – 2 Corinthians 10:4-6

10 – Ephesians 4:15

CHAPTER 6

Soul Ties

Testimony

"My mother passed away and I couldn't get over
her death, though I knew she was with Jesus.
I am now 100 percent healed after receiving inner
healing and deliverance."

Whenever we are in a relationship with someone, whether on a casual basis or a deeper level, soul ties are formed. In its simplest form, a soul tie joins two souls together in the spiritual realm. They bind, fasten, and secure one soul to another. The Bible doesn't use the words "soul tie" but states that we become one flesh with whomever we are joined to.[1]

Soul ties create tendencies and desires within us that can be good or bad. They can pull us toward God or away from him. Consider someone who is born and raised in the church but becomes involved with someone who has no desire for the things of God. More often than not, the Christian will turn away from God, rather than the other person choosing a relationship with God.

Scripture teaches that there are godly soul ties and ungodly ones. Soul ties not only bind two souls together, they unite the spirits and bodies of those involved as well. They can occur in relationships such as those between friends, co-workers, church members, brothers and sisters, parents and children, and husbands and wives. Let's look at an example of a soul tie that develops between a man and a woman as their relationship deepens:

When a man and woman first meet, they primarily relate through words, with only superficial connection. If they continue to talk and they decide they like each other, they begin to form a *soul tie*. There is a connection forming between them that goes deeper that what is seen on the surface. When they start to date and share their hopes, dreams, emotions, and future, they deepen their soul tie because they now have an emotional bond. If these people are Christians and they start praying together, they develop a *spiritual tie* because they are relating on a spiritual level. If this couple chooses to marry, they form a *physical tie* as they join themselves in a sexual union.

Godly Soul Ties

The Israelites understood that when they entered into "covenant" with someone, they were joining their bodies, souls, and spirits with that person. Covenants can be considered soul ties. Depending on the type of covenant entered into, there can be an exchange of blood, clothing, weaponry, a meal, or names; and/or the participants may build a memorial as a witness to their bond. The Bible contains examples of godly soul ties:

David and Jonathan

We read of a covenant soul tie made between David and Jonathan before David became king of Israel:

"And it came to pass, when he had made an end of speaking unto Saul, that the soul of Jonathan was knit with the soul of David, and Jonathan loved him as his own soul" (1 Samuel 18:1).

The words "knit" and "cleave" mean to *cling or adhere to, abide (fast) together.*[2] When love between two people comes from their hearts, the soul tie between them benefits both parties. Jesus spoke of this kind of love.

"Greater love hath no man than this, that a man lay down his life for his friends" (John 15:13). David and Jonathan exemplified this type of love.

Naomi and Ruth

The book of Ruth gives another example of a godly soul tie. Naomi had lost her husband and both sons while in the country of Moab, and wanted to return to her home in Israel. She told both of her daughters-in-law to stay in Moab. Orpah did so, but Ruth said:

Intreat me not to leave thee, or to return from following after thee: for whither thou goest, I will go; and where thou lodgest, I will lodge: thy people shall be my people, and thy God my God: Where thou diest, will I die, and there will I be buried: the LORD do so to me, and more also, if ought but death part thee and me.

Ruth 1:16-17

Naomi and Ruth had spent ten years together. They must have developed a very deep mother-in-law/daughter-in-law soul tie relationship for Ruth to choose to stay with Naomi and forsake her own country.

Marriage

The love Jesus talked about in the book of John is also the type of soul tie that forms the foundation of a strong and healthy marriage, one that will endure the tests and trials that inevitably come.[3]

"Therefore shall a man leave his father and his mother, and shall cleave unto his wife: and they shall be one flesh" (Genesis 2:24).

Jesus repeated this on two occasions.[4]

Two are better than one; because they have a good reward for their labour. For if they fall, the one will lift up his fellow: but woe to him that is alone when he falleth; for he hath not another to help him up. Again, if two lie together, then they have heat: but how can one be warm alone? And if one prevail against him, two shall withstand him; and a threefold cord is not quickly broken.

Ecclesiastes 4:9-12

The stronger the bond or soul tie between a husband and wife, the longer their relationship will last. The physical, emotional, and mental strengths of one will sustain the other in times of adversity, and they will rejoice together in times of triumph. The Lord highly honors the marriage relationship and the resulting soul ties because it exemplifies his love for the Church. Paul relates marriage to the "profound mystery" of Christ's relationship with the Church.[5] Thus we see that God instituted soul ties for the benefit of mankind.

Christ and the Church

The blood Christ shed at Calvary created a soul tie between himself and those who accept his finished work. Christ's blood brought us into right relationship with God. It allows us to be part of his family. We are in a covenant soul tie relationship with him that cannot be broken unless we choose to walk away from it.

Testimony

"I felt greater peace after the second session and
I am thankful for the excellent teaching on
demon affliction and deliverance."

Ungodly Soul Ties

Whatever God creates for our benefit and blessing, Satan wants to pervert and curse. This is true of soul ties as well. Ungodly soul ties can form inappropriate male/male, female/female, or male/female relationships through spending too much time together, flirting, or sharing personal struggles—whether at work, church, or other places people interact.

One of the deepest soul ties we can form comes through sexual union. It involves the bodies, souls, and spirits of those involved. We share our bodies and emotions. Our spirits become united because God created sexual intimacy to be a foundational part of the marriage covenant.

God has designed most women to come under the protection, care, and authority of a man. When a man has sex with her, he sometimes gains a form of dominion over her.

"Unto the woman he said, I will greatly multiply thy sorrow and thy conception; in sorrow thou shalt bring forth children; and thy desire shall be to thy husband, and he shall rule [have dominion] over thee" (Genesis 3:16, brackets added).

Because the sexual relationship between a man and a woman involves body, soul, and spirit, Satan desires to entice and deceive us into sin in this area. *Any* sexual union (physical, fantasy, or otherwise) that is not with our spouse will always create an ungodly soul tie. The intimate bond formed with another person cannot be blessed by God.

"Ye have heard that it was said by them of old time, Thou shalt not commit adultery: But I say unto you, That whosoever looketh on a woman to lust after her hath committed adultery with her already in his heart" (Matthew 5:27-28).

Paul addresses sexual immorality and the effects it has on us.[6] He points out that we become "one flesh" when we have sex with a prostitute (male or female), but this soul tie also extends to anyone we have sex with outside of marriage.

Dinah and Shechem

And Dinah the daughter of Leah, which she bare unto Jacob, went out to see the daughters of the land. And when Shechem the son of Hamor the Hivite, prince of the country, saw her, he took her, and lay with her, and defiled her. And his soul clave unto Dinah the daughter of Jacob, and he loved the damsel, and spake kindly unto the damsel.

Genesis 34:1-3

71

In this story, Shechem, a Hivite, lusted after Dinah, an Israelite, and raped her, forming an ungodly soul tie between the two. When Jacob and his sons found out, they were furious and deceived Shechem, his father Hamor, and all males from their city, asking them to be circumcised so the two nations could intermarry (including Shechem and Dinah). Three days into the rite of circumcision, while all the Hivite males were still incapacitated, two of Jacob's sons, Levi and Simeon, went into the Hivite town and killed all the men present, including Hamor and Shechem.

Although these consequences are extreme, they represent a sobering point: Most sexual involvement outside of marriage will form an ungodly soul tie that can potentially destroy marriages, families, friendships, and even individual lives. God has set into place both natural and spiritual laws that bring either blessing when obeyed or cursing when ignored. Just as marriage forms a godly soul tie that brings blessing, adultery and fornication form ungodly soul ties that invoke bondage and enslavement.

Characteristics of Ungodly Soul Ties

A careful examination of our relationships will reveal godly and ungodly soul ties. We need to ask ourselves, "Does this relationship glorify God? Is it bringing me closer to Jesus?"

Just because we have a relationship with another Christian does not necessarily mean there is a godly soul tie formed. Here are some questions to ask ourselves:

- Do you feel you are compromising or being compromised in ways that go against your conscience or God's Word?
- Is the relationship one-sided or self-centered?
- Is there mutual sharing, growth, and freedom? Or is there bondage, control, and manipulation?
- Are the fruits of the Spirit exhibited in the relationship?
- Does the relationship move you toward or away from God?

When impure motives or self-centeredness are at the core of a relationship, the soul tie formed can lead to manipulation and abuse. One person can actually control another through an ungodly soul tie, because the minds of the two are open to one another, and the enemy has a legal right to wreak havoc on the relationship.

Breaking Ungodly Soul Ties

Although ungodly soul ties are sinful, the good news is that Jesus forgives *all* sin.

"If we confess our sins, he is faithful and just to forgive us our sins, and to cleanse us from all unrighteousness" (1 John 1:9).

We need to break the unhealthy soul ties we have made with other people regardless of how they were formed. Breaking these is similar to a mother who, after giving birth to her child, allows the umbilical cord that ties the two together to be cut. When this happens, the baby can start its new life and begin to grow on its own. In the same way, it is important that we cut and sever all ungodly soul ties so we can move on with our lives. As long as we continue to have ungodly soul ties in our lives, we will not be free to pursue healthy relationships.

Breaking ungodly soul ties involves three important steps: prayer, a willful decision, and walking away.

In our personal time with God, we ask him to show us any ungodly relationships we may be involved in. We then ask his forgiveness for our involvement, break and renounce each soul tie formed, and cover them in the blood of Jesus. If we are unsure about particular relationships, talking to a trusted friend, pastor, or counselor will help us make a godly decision.

Through acts of our wills, we then mentally *choose* to leave the ungodly relationships. This is often the hardest part. There has to be an agreement within our wills, or we will not end the relationships.[7] If we are struggling to agree with this, we need to find out what benefits we are receiving by staying in the relationships. As paradoxical as this may sound, even in an abusive relationship, the abused person is benefitting in some way.

Finally, we must physically walk away from the ungodly relationships. If possible, we should talk with the other person involved. We should avoid blame but take responsibility for our parts, being as honest as possible. The other person may or may not agree, and there may be emotional pain and disappointment involved. However, for our own spiritual growth and peace of mind, we should end the relationships as soon as possible.

"Wherefore come out from among them, and be ye separate, saith the Lord, and touch not the unclean thing; and I will receive you, And will be a Father unto you, and ye shall be my sons and daughters, saith the Lord Almighty" (2 Corinthians 6:17-18).

When God leads us to break a soul tie, we can trust him to draw us closer to himself in response to our obedience and to help us develop new godly relationships and soul ties.

Testimony

"I had the pleasure of going through the seminar and being set free from a spirit of fear that had plagued me from the time I was 9 years old."

Chapter 6 Soul Ties

1 – Matthew 19:5; Genesis 2:24; 1Corinthians 6:16-17
2 – Genesis 2:24
3 – John 15:13
4 – Matthew 19:5, Mark 10:7
5 – Ephesians 5:22-33
6 – 1 Corinthians 6:12-20
7 – Amos 3:3

CHAPTER 7

Spoken Vows and Inner Vows

Inner vows can be called "self-made promises." These are promises made in reaction to someone else's words or actions. They may or may not be verbalized. Inner vows are concrete, black-and-white expressions of our will characterized by words such as *I will/I won't; you always/you never;* or *I never will again*. Often they are made early in life in reaction to words, actions, or behaviors of someone significant in our lives. More commonly, they have negative connotations, although there are many examples of positive inner vows.

It is commonly understood that making a vow is usually not a good practice. Even good vows place the emphasis on oneself, not God. They often have negative consequences in our lives or the lives of others.

> Again, ye have heard that it hath been said by them of old time, Thou shalt not forswear thyself, but shalt perform unto the Lord thine oaths: But I say unto you, Swear not at all; neither by heaven; for it is God's throne: Nor by the earth; for it is his footstool: neither by Jerusalem; for it is the city of the great King. Neither shalt thou swear by thy head, because thou canst not make one hair white or black. But let your communication be, Yea, yea; Nay, nay: for whatsoever is more than these cometh of evil.
>
> Matthew 5:33-37

James tells us not to swear by heaven or earth, but let our yes be yes and our no be no.[1] Ecclesiastes tells us to:

> Keep thy foot when thou goest to the house of God, and be more ready to hear, than to give the sacrifice of fools: for they consider not that they do evil. Be not rash with thy mouth, and let not thine heart be hasty to utter any thing before God: for God is in heaven, and thou upon earth: therefore let thy words be few. For a dream cometh through the multitude of business; and a fool's voice is known by multitude of words. When thou vowest a vow unto God, defer not to pay it; for he hath no pleasure in fools: pay that which thou hast vowed. Better is it that thou shouldest not vow, than that thou shouldest vow and not pay. Suffer not thy mouth to cause thy flesh to sin; neither say thou before the angel, that it was an error: wherefore should God be angry at thy voice, and destroy the work of thine hands? For in the multitude of dreams and many words there are also divers vanities: but fear thou God.
>
> Ecclesiastes 5:1-7

The above verses show that making vows creates traps that can enslave us and that vows do not glorify God in any way. The reasons are many:

- Vows concern our behavior in the future, and the future is something we have little control over.
- Vows can allow the enemy to gain a foothold in our lives.
- Vows can be made in order to entice, deceive, and cheat others.
- Breaking a vow can result in judgment upon ourselves, causing destruction in our lives.
- We may make a vow dependent upon someone else who is unable to keep his or her word, such as obligating him or her to perform a task.
- Sometimes the circumstances in our lives change and we cannot keep the vows we have made.
- Negative vows create negative focuses and tendencies that work against us in the spirit world.

Testimony

"Had I not gone through the seminar, I would have
spent my life as a defeated Christian, powerless,
and a target for every defeat."

Foolish Vows

In biblical times, vows were sacred; they were kept no matter what the consequence. There are a number of foolish vows recorded:

Herod and His Daughter

In Matthew we read of a vow that Herod the Tetrarch made to his stepdaughter concerning John the Baptist:

> But when Herod's birthday was kept, the daughter of Herodias danced before them, and pleased Herod. Whereupon he promised with an oath to give her whatsoever she would ask. And she, being before instructed of her mother, said, Give me here John Baptist's head in a charger. And the king was sorry: nevertheless for the oath's sake, and them which sat with him at meat, he commanded it to be given her. And he sent, and beheaded John in the prison. And his head was brought in a charger, and given to the damsel: and she brought it to her mother. And his disciples came, and took up the body, and buried it, and went and told Jesus.
>
> Matthew 14:6-12

Herod made an open vow to his stepdaughter. When he heard her reply, he was filled with regret—but he had to keep his word or lose face with those who were attending his banquet.

SPIRITUAL WARFARE

The Jewish Assassins

The book of Acts records a vow made by some Jewish assassins who bound themselves with an absolute oath not to eat or drink until they had killed Paul. If they truly had kept their oath (the Bible does not record whether or not they did) they would have starved to death, because Paul was rescued.[2] Their oath depended on future circumstances, which they had little control over.

Jephthah's Daughter

Judges records the story of Jephthah's foolish vow that resulted in his daughter's death. This tragic oath came about because it was open-ended:

Then the Spirit of the LORD came upon Jephthah, and he passed over Gilead, and Manasseh, and passed over Mizpeh of Gilead, and from Mizpeh of Gilead he passed over unto the children of Ammon. And Jephthah vowed a vow unto the LORD, and said, If thou shalt without fail deliver the children of Ammon into mine hands, Then it shall be, that whatsoever cometh forth of the doors of my house to meet me, when I return in peace from the children of Ammon, shall surely be the LORD's, and I will offer it up for a burnt offering. So Jephthah passed over unto the children of Ammon to fight against them; and the LORD delivered them into his hands. And he smote them from Aroer, even till thou come to Minnith, even twenty cities, and unto the plain of the vineyards, with a very great slaughter. Thus the children of Ammon were subdued before the children of Israel. And Jephthah came to Mizpeh unto his house, and, behold, his daughter came out to meet him with timbrels and with dances: and she was his only child; beside her he had neither son nor daughter. And it came to pass, when he saw her, that he rent his clothes, and said, Alas, my daughter! thou hast brought me very low, and thou art one of them that trouble me: for I have opened my mouth unto the LORD, and I cannot go back. And she said unto him, My father, if thou hast opened thy mouth unto the LORD, do to me according to that which hath proceeded out of thy mouth; forasmuch as the LORD hath taken vengeance for thee of thine enemies, even of the children of Ammon. And she said unto her father, Let this thing be done for me: let me alone two months, that I may go up and down upon the mountains, and bewail my virginity, I and my fellows. And he said, Go. And he sent her away for two months: and she went with her companions, and bewailed her virginity upon the mountains. And it came to pass at the end of two months, that she returned unto her father, who did with her according to his vow which he had vowed: and she knew no man. And it was a custom in Israel, That the daughters of Israel went yearly to lament the daughter of Jephthah the Gileadite four days in a year.

Judges 11:29-40

From the above examples, we see that vows can bring judgment and tragic consequences into our lives and the lives of others—even for those who are innocent.

Testimony

"I am more focused, have a greater understanding of spiritual matters, and now experience greater peace, love, compassion, and understanding."

The Nature of Inner Vows

As adults we can recognize things we said as children that were foolish and renounce them, giving no further thought to our words.

"When I was a child; I spake as a child, I understood as a child, I thought as a child: but when I became a man, I put away childish things" (1 Corinthians 13:11).

For instance, as children we may have been shy, insecure, selfish, demanding, or forgetful. But as we grew into adulthood, we outgrew these characteristics. We may now say, "When I was a child I was a bully, but I'm not that way any longer."

Childhood vows are not absolutes, but they create tendencies that have the ability to directly affect our behavior. What separates inner vows from behavioral changes is that the inner vows *never* change, no matter our age; they are not governed by normal maturing. For instance, as children we might say, "I hate my mom; I'll never be like her," then set about making sure our behavior never matches our mothers'. The problem is that the hatred we felt toward our mother actually *binds* us to her. As adults, we may exhibit characteristics that are similar to our mothers', and our hatred will become *self-hatred*. Even if we decide to change our behavior, our childhood vows still bind us to whatever characteristics we hated in our mothers. This can set up a vicious cycle of hatred and self-hatred that stunts our maturity and that can be broken only through prayerful renunciation and forgiveness.

Often, inner vows do not show up in our lives until later. For instance, as children we may say, "I will never become an alcoholic like my dad" or "When I get older I will get even with him." The bitter roots we create when we make such a vow may not manifest themselves in immediate behavior but can take effect later in life. The vows may lie dormant until triggered by the right person and/or situation. We may not even remember the vows until they take effect.

Renouncing Inner Vows

We have all made inner vows of varying intensity and meaning. Inner vows are as common to children as cars are to their parents. Some vows are good and others destructive. Even the good vows need to be released so we are not subject to our flesh but led into freedom by the Spirit.

Sometimes merely seeing and breaking inner vows will set us free. Once the Holy Spirit has revealed inner vows, we must confess them, renounce them, and take authority over them in the name of Jesus in order to break their power. But some vows develop deep roots within our souls that may remain after the original vow has been broken. These types of vows build strongholds and bondages in our lives, seeking to fulfill their original intent. They seek to hide who we truly are in order to guard us from further pain.

Inner vows can form a protective web of deceit over childhood pain. Such webs can entangle us in indifference, ambivalence, uncaring attitudes, developing hearts of stone, harboring unforgiveness, evasive and defensive mechanisms, deep-seated anger, using extreme words (always/never), and anxieties and fears that make trusting another individual difficult. Even after we have renounced inner vows, we must create new thought patterns to replace the old. Extended inner healing and/or counseling may be necessary in order to completely root out all layers of such vows.

Inner vows are as varied at the people who utter them. For example, a young woman may swear she will never go on an airplane due to an inner vow as a child to never risk doing something she cannot control. A man may fear emotional intimacy because he was embarrassed by a girl in front of his friends in grade school.

We may make vows never to be seen in public, vows that reinforce our belief systems ("I am so stupid!"), vows that limit our ability to receive praise or commendation from others, vows that keep us from intimacy. For instance, we may say:

"I'll never let it happen to me again."

"I'll never fail again."

"I'll be the best ever."

"I'll never try again."

"I am not going to grow up."

"I'll be strong."

"No one is going to rule me."

Such statements are good indicators that we have been deeply hurt.

As children, we may make powerful statements against our parents that end up ruining our lives and destroying relationships. Some inner vows are triggered by fear, others by physical or emotional pain. They may be disguised as oaths we choose to make that can control different aspects of our behavior. Childhood and adult vows are similar in nature, but they differ in that childhood vows can be hidden in the subconscious for many years. If a boy says to himself, "I'll get even with her," (his mother or sister), he may later project this same vow onto all women who enter his life. A girl may say, "I'll never let him (brother or father) get the best of me again," which may result in defensive reactions and overt anger toward her husband.

Some inner vows set us up for continual failure.

"I'll never let my temper go again. Nothing good comes about when I do."

Such a vow will lead us into cycles of self-criticism, self-rejection, and setting standards for ourselves that are impossible to meet. This further leads to repressed anger, which can be set off by an innocent comment from another person. A vow such as, "I'll never again be caught unprepared when asked a question," can drive us into anxiety and fear of public speaking, or even hold us back from a job promotion.

How do we find the inner vows we have made? By asking the Holy Spirit for revelation and guidance. Inner vows can be the roots of stubborn habits and patterns in our lives. Compulsive behavior may cover up an inner vow. The Holy Spirit can guide us to uncover hidden inner vows and show us their effects on our present-day struggles. We must also remember that inner vows often work in conjunction with bitter root judgments and hidden sins such as unforgiveness, resentment, and fear.

Only when we know our authority in Christ can we break vows and resist the strongholds they have had on our lives. We must understand their harmful effects and be convicted by the Holy Spirit that they are truly sin. No matter what we proclaim, actions—not words—will reveal whether or not we want to rid ourselves of our inner vows.

It takes time before the fruits of broken vows are evident in our lives, and time will tell how determined we are to resist the inner vows. Even this step cannot be taken without empowerment from the Holy Spirit. Therefore, our prayer lives are of utmost importance. Understanding and receiving forgiveness, acceptance, and love from the Holy Spirit is key to breaking inner vows and maintaining new habits and patterns. Once exposed and dealt with, inner vows will fall away either instantly or over time. However, changing old habits and behaviors takes time. Patience is needed so that we can learn how to walk in newness of life.

Testimony

"I spent the last fifteen years of life in fear of being raped
and beaten.
However, now I'm totally free. Deliverance truly works."

"I went back through life forgiving each and every person
the Holy Spirit showed me.
My relationship with my father was restored after
18 years.
I'm not an angry person anymore."

Chapter 7 Inner Vows

1 – James 5:12
2 – Acts 23:20-24

CHAPTER 8

Giving and Receiving Forgiveness

"You want me to forgive him after what he has done? Are you kidding me?" "How could God forgive me after what I've done? I'm rotten to the core. I can never forgive myself."

As pastors we hear statements like these almost every day from Christians. This is tragic. People put themselves in bondage and expose themselves to Satan's lies and attacks because they do not understand the principles of forgiveness. Instead they choose to hold onto unforgiveness, a yoke and stronghold that blunts their ability to love and accept others, cripples friendships, destroys marriages, and can lead to diseases and psychosomatic illnesses in the spirit, soul, and body.

The Meaning of Forgiveness

At the outset, Jesus proclaimed forgiveness as a basis of his ministry. From the time he taught his disciples to pray through to his last words before dying, Jesus proclaimed the power, importance, and necessity of forgiving others.[1]

The dictionary defines forgiveness as *a mental, emotional and/or spiritual process of ceasing to feel resentment, indignation or anger against another person for a perceived offense, difference or mistake, or ceasing to demand punishment or restitution.*

In *Strong's Concordance*, the Hebrew word "kaphar" is the root for forgiveness. Kaphar means *to cover, expiate or condone, placate or cancel, appease, make (an atonement, cleanse, disannul, forgive, be merciful, pacify, pardon, purge (away), put off, or reconcile (make reconciliation).* In the New Testament, forgiveness is translated from various Greek words that mean *to free fully, relieve, release, dismiss, pardon, forgive, let go, loose, release, set at liberty; lay aside, to grant as a favor, i.e. gratuitously, in kindness, pardon or rescue: deliver, (frankly) forgive, (freely) give, grant.*

When Jesus hung on the cross he prayed, "Father, forgive them; for they know not what they do."[2] Consider for a moment what he was really doing. We say, "I'll forgive my dad if he changes." Or, "I'll forgive my coworker if he asks my forgiveness or apologizes." But Jesus did not make his forgiveness conditional: He chose to forgive. He forgave his offenders

1. while they were doing the very thing for which he was forgiving them;
2. even though they hadn't changed;
3. though they hadn't asked his forgiveness;
4. though they were still inflicting pain upon him to the point of death;
5. unconditionally;
6. and asked the Father to forgive them as well.

Willingness to forgive is absolutely essential in our lives, and forgiveness must be an integral part of our lifestyles. Remember, forgiveness has the word "give" in the middle of it. This means forgiveness is a *gift*: It is not something we earn or deserve.

There are some fallacies concerning what forgiveness entails. Forgiveness is not

- justifying or excusing someone's behavior;
- forgetting, nor does the passing of time lead us to "forgive and forget";
- denying our emotional woundedness, pretending that "it wasn't such a big deal" or acting as if the offense never happened;
- asking God to forgive someone (although it may be part of the process);

- always confrontational (this also may be part of the process).

The Bondage of Unforgiveness

Our fallen nature causes us to be easily offended and hold onto offenses. Thus, Jesus addressed the issue of unforgiveness:

"And forgive us our debts, as we forgive our debtors. ... For if ye forgive men their trespasses, your heavenly Father will also forgive you: But if ye forgive not men their trespasses, neither will your Father forgive your trespasses" (Matthew 6:12, 14-15).

When someone offends us, we want to defend ourselves and make the other person pay. We feel he or she *owes* us. To forgive would mean releasing someone from his or her indebtedness to us—something we are loath to do. However, when we hold onto unforgiveness, we open ourselves up to the enemy's attacks, we hinder our prayer lives, and we expose our bodies to negative chemical reactions that can lead to debilitating diseases and long-term illnesses.

The Tormentors

Unforgiveness can open a door for torment within our lives. Jesus illustrates this in the parable of the unmerciful servant.[3] The servant owed a great sum of money to a certain king and begged the king to have patience with him until he could pay his debt. The king was moved with compassion and forgave him the debt. But the same servant went out and found one of his fellow servants who owed him a much smaller debt. The first servant grabbed the second and demanded payment. When his fellow servant could not pay, he was thrown into jail. When the king found out, he said:

O thou wicked servant, I forgave thee all that debt, because thou desiredst me: Shouldest not thou also have had compassion on thy fellowservant, even as I had pity on thee? And his lord was wroth, and delivered him to the tormentors, till he should pay all that was due unto him. So likewise shall my heavenly Father do also unto you, if ye from your hearts forgive not every one his brother their trespasses.

Matthew 18:32-35

Choosing *not* to forgive gives demons legal access to our lives. They are the tormentors in this passage of Scripture, tormenting and torturing us with hatred, envy, strife, division, and anger. God is not the author of torment. The servant was wicked—he would not forgive his fellow servant. We are God's "servants" today. When we break "spiritual law" through unforgiveness, we can be delivered to the tormentors.

Unanswered Prayer

Have you ever wondered why some of your prayers are not answered? Unforgiveness could be a reason.

Jesus said, "Therefore I say unto you, what things soever ye desire, when ye pray, believe that ye receive them, and ye shall have them. And when ye stand praying, forgive, if ye have ought against any: that your Father also which is in heaven may forgive you your trespasses" (Mark 11:24-25).

In addressing husbands, Peter states that men are to learn to honor and accept their wives, for wives are joint heirs in this life. Failing to do so leads to a husband's prayers being hindered.[4]

Jesus wants us to build relationships with God, each other, and ourselves. But unforgiveness tears down relationships, builds walls of division, and blocks our ability to hear truth from God and others.

Defilement

Unforgiveness is the ground in which a root of bitterness grows and "defiles many."[5] Unforgiveness feeds bitterness, resentment, hatred, anger, malice, discord, slander, and gossip, spreading them into the hearts of others. Have you ever walked into work after having an argument at home and blown up at a coworker? Even when we try to hide or deny our feelings, they always find a way to sneak out—usually when we least expect them to. But if we learn to forgive, we can rid ourselves of many forms of emotional bondage.

Satan's Foothold

"To whom ye forgive any thing, I forgive also: for if I forgave any thing, to whom I forgave it, for your sakes forgave I it in the person of Christ; Lest Satan should get an advantage of us: for we are not ignorant of his devices" (2 Corinthians 2:10-11).

Demons can affect our lives only to the extent that they have a legal right to enter. Satan is the father of unforgiveness. When we hold onto it, he has a legal right to inflict our minds with his fiery darts, further compounding the ugly thoughts and feelings we have been dwelling on.

Excuses and Defense Mechanisms

Often, we do not recognize when we are holding onto unforgiveness. Here are indicating statements:
- I'll forgive but never forget.
- I just couldn't respect my father.
- I don't hate him, I just don't like him.
- He'll never learn if I keep making it easy for him.
- I can never forgive my _____ for what he/she/they did to me.
- I forgive you, but I don't want to deal with it.
- I'll forgive you, but I don't want anything to do with you. Stay away from me!
- I'm tired of this. I'm not going to keep forgiving you until *you* pray about it by seeking God and truly repenting. Come back when you finally get it right.

We can also hold onto unforgiveness for the following reasons:
1. Pride—forgiving others makes me look weak.
2. Control—we can manipulate others.
3. Fear—we might be hurt again.
4. Pain—if we ignore someone, we won't hurt inside anymore.
5. Revenge—we want others to pay for what they did to us.

6. Confusion—we don't fully understand and accept God's love and forgiveness for ourselves.

7. Self-loathing—we choose not to forgive ourselves. Therefore we cannot truly forgive others.

8. Bitterness—it seems too easy and unfair; we are overlooking or condoning another's sin.

Unforgiveness is often the root behind many of our defense mechanisms. We hide behind the defense mechanisms, thinking they will protect us from further hurt. These include the following:

- exaggerating or bragging
- rationalizing and excuse-making
- excessive shyness
- perfectionism
- attention-getting
- compulsive work or busyness
- repressed feelings and indifference
- lack of communication or silent treatment
- nervous and/or obsessive-compulsive habits
- a critical or negative attitude
- overzealous religious activity
- overcompensation
- trouble with authority
- superficial relationships
- sarcasm
- outbursts of anger
- using humor as a cover to keep people from getting too close
- running away from problems or pressures

Defense mechanisms are the same as putting a bandage on an infected wound. It seems like it is helping, but the infection continues to fester. The bandage must be taken off, and the cut cleaned out and allowed to heal. We must acknowledge that our defenses are covering pain hidden in our hearts. The unforgiveness is festering within.

"If we confess our sins, he is faithful and just to forgive us our sins, and to cleanse us from all unrighteousness" (1 John 1:9).

Second Greatest Commandment

Jesus stated that the second greatest command is to love our neighbor in the same way that we love ourselves:

"And the second is like, namely this, Thou shalt love thy neighbour as thyself. There is none other commandment greater than these" (Mark 12:31).

There is a principle in this Scripture that is rarely taught: we cannot love our neighbor more than we love ourselves. The remarkable thing is we *really do* love our neighbor as ourselves. We hold others to the same standards we hold ourselves to. Our hatred of others can often be traced back to a hatred of self. If we are kind, forgiving, or benevolent towards others, we treat ourselves in the same respect. When we hold unforgiveness towards others, we are often harsh and berating toward ourselves. We don't think we deserve to be forgiven.

Testimony

"I no longer have to take tranquilizers or antidepressants.
I haven't had any anxiety; I'm calm and peaceful."

Principles of Forgiveness

Forgiving others can be difficult because we anguish over extending grace toward those who have hurt us. To release a person instead of exacting punishment requires us to reach out in love instead of demanding what we think we are owed.

Forgiving others is contrary to our natural inclinations. Forgiveness is not forgetting the wrong that was done. Forgiveness itself does not remove the emotional pain we feel. But it is the first step toward emotional healing. Remember, forgiveness is first an act of our will, not a feeling. We can choose to forgive even if we don't feel like it because it is within our power to do so.

When we choose to forgive someone in the name of Jesus, it is done. Finished! This is important to understand and believe. We do not have

93

to forgive the person for the same incident over and over. It is a decision we can make in prayer, then in person. Forgiveness can be instantaneous or a process. The issue is not whether we *feel* like forgiving but whether we *choose* to forgive. If we choose to be willing, God promises to give us the desire to change. God has forgiven our sins and asks us to follow his example. He wants us to forgive others and ourselves when we feel we have been wronged. There are times when we must even "forgive" God because we feel he has been unjust or allowed situations into our lives that may have resulted in harm. Forgiving God does not mean he has done something wrong. We are simply releasing the unforgiveness we have harbored against him.

Reconciliation

"And all things are of God, who hath reconciled us to himself by Jesus Christ, and hath given to us the ministry of reconciliation; To wit, that God was in Christ, reconciling the world unto himself, not imputing their trespasses unto them; and hath committed unto us the word of reconciliation" (2 Corinthians 5:18-19).

Because God is most concerned about relationships, he has given every believer the ministry of reconciliation. We are to reconcile unbelievers to God through Jesus Christ and reconcile relationships between believers through giving and receiving forgiveness.

Sowing and Reaping

Jesus talks about the importance of forgiving others.

"For if ye forgive men their trespasses, your heavenly Father will also forgive you: But if ye forgive not men their trespasses, neither will your Father forgive your trespasses" (Mathew 6:14-15).

This is an example of the law of sowing and reaping. Unforgiveness will always come back upon us in increasing measure, binding us further in its bitter shackles.

To break this vicious cycle, Paul exhorts us to forbear and forgive those who have quarrels against us, even as Christ forgave us.[6] When we remind ourselves of the price Jesus paid for our sins, we can offer forgiveness to others from our hearts.

Freeing the Captives

The Bible states we are all sinners: "For all have sinned, and come short of the glory of God" (Romans 3:23). When Jesus hung on the cross, he paid the full penalty for our sin: "Being justified freely by his grace through the redemption that is in Christ Jesus" (Romans 3:24).

When we forgive others, we are acting like our Heavenly Father. Yet we may still struggle to forgive because we feel the offending party is getting away without any penalty. We must remember we are forgiving their *sin* and may choose to absolve them of their consequences and responsibilities. Forgiveness doesn't mean we look the other way. Nor does it mean there are no consequences for the wrongs committed against us (or the wrongs we commit against others).

The universal law of sowing and reaping is brought into effect whenever there is sin. For instance, if I steal something and am arrested, the person from whom I stole may forgive me, but a judge can still sentence me to probation or jail.

Why then does the Bible place such a strong emphasis on the need to forgive? When we forgive others we are freeing *ourselves* from the bitterness and anguish that hold us in bondage. Even if the other person does not admit his or her wrongdoing, forgiving him or her is paramount for our own mental and spiritual health. Thus, when we forgive others, we are the ones who benefit the most. In situations where the other person admits his or her sin and asks for forgiveness, reconciliation can occur.[7]

Testimony

"After the seminar, I felt drained and physically
exhausted but free!
Sunday morning I entered into the presence of the Lord
with no hindrances."

95

Forgiveness and Feelings

When God forgave us through the death and resurrection of his son, he did so as an act of his will—he chose to forgive. But Jesus still suffered feelings of rejection.

"And when the sixth hour was come, there was darkness over the whole land until the ninth hour. And at the ninth hour Jesus cried with a loud voice, saying, Eloi, Eloi, lama sabachthani? which is, being interpreted, My God, my God, why hast thou forsaken me?" (Mark 15:33-34).

> *Oftentimes, when there is no confrontation, we are tempted to gossip about the offense committed against us.*

In the same way, when we forgive others we do so as an act of our wills, regardless of how we feel about the situations or the people involved. What, then, do we do with our feelings? We do not deny or negate them. We admit how we truly feel, and we work through our feelings until we reach a point where we can release them to God. The best way we have found to process and release feelings is through inner healing. Whether on your own or with an experienced counselor, inner healing prayer removes the pain attached to each memory that has resulted from a particular offense.

Forgiveness and Confrontation

Forgiving someone does not mean we *never* confront the offending party. Nor does it mean we *always* confront. When to confront someone comes down to examining our hearts before God. Oftentimes, when there is no confrontation, we are tempted to gossip about the offense committed against us. We feel hurt and want someone else to validate and justify our feelings.

For most of us, confrontation is scary. We don't like confrontation because it often stirs up feelings of rejection. But the Bible teaches us that we should confront because it can lead to healed relationships. "Therefore if thou bring thy gift to the altar, and there rememberest that thy brother hath ought against thee; Leave there thy gift before the altar, and go thy way; first be reconciled to thy brother, and then come and offer thy gift." (Matthew 5:23-24). Jesus said, "Moreover if thy brother shall trespass against thee, go and tell him his fault between thee and him alone: if he shall hear thee, thou hast gained thy brother" (Matthew 18:15).

The key to confrontation is to "speak the truth in love."[8] We must learn how to keep confrontations objective, not subjective. We need to stay focused on the issues and not make the confrontations personal. The offending people are not *bad*, but the offenses committed against us were hurtful. We must separate people from their offending words or actions. Doing so will keep us from attacking the other people's character and stop us from making the issues personal.

Testimony

"I am more at peace with myself than
I have ever been in my entire life.
I sleep well; no more tossing and turning."

Forgiveness and Responsibility

Does forgiving someone absolve him or her of his or her responsibility? In most cases, no. Only if we choose to release a person is he or she free of his or her obligations. For instance, if someone took a pen from me and I found out, I might say, "It's okay, you can keep it." Conversely, if I were sexually abused as a child, I may forgive the perpetrator, but that doesn't mean he or she will not go to jail. Jesus forgave the thief on the cross when he asked him to, but he didn't say, "You are free to go now. Step down from your cross."

Whether or not a person is released from personal responsibility depends largely on the offense committed and our willingness to let go of any recompense. But when we seek retribution, we must also check our hearts:

- Have we truly forgiven, or are we holding the offending party responsible because we want him or her to pay?

- What lessons will be learned by holding someone responsible for his or her actions?
- What is God saying?

These are questions that need to be weighed before making a decision to hold someone accountable.

Although forgiveness may seem to be a complicated issue, it doesn't have to be. God tells us to forgive. Period. Forgiveness becomes complicated only when we choose to look at it through our own eyes and deal with offenses our own ways. We must learn how to forgive God's way—freely and completely. Forgiving others as God has forgiven us brings healing and wholeness, and develops Christlike character. And these are things God desires us all to have.

Chapter 8 Forgiveness

1 – Matthew 6:12-15; Luke 23:34
2 – Luke 23:34
3 – Matthew 18:22-35
4 – 1 Peter 3:7
5 – Hebrews 12:15
6 – Colossians 3:12-13
7 – 2 Corinthians 5:19
8 – Ephesians 4:15

CHAPTER 9

The Process of Personal Inner Healing

Testimony

"I appreciated the inner healing session. It was awesome
having the Holy Spirit walk back in time with me to
various traumatic experiences in my life, then
have Jesus heal the memories."

Scripture clearly states God wants to heal our broken hearts and
our wounded souls. However, the words "inner healing" can spark
debate among Christians, with many claiming it is "new age" terminology. Some prefer "soul healing," "healing the brokenhearted," or similar names. However, no matter the title used, one thing is clear: The fruit
of this ministry cannot be denied.[1]

When we receive freedom through inner healing—which in reality is specific and targeted prayer—the Holy Spirit removes the pain
embedded in particular memories that have harmful effects in our lives.
The effects of generational sins, soul ties, curses, inner vows, and bitter
root judgments can also be addressed during this time. After God brings
healing, the memory itself remains but the emotional pain does not.
Once individual memories are healed, our conscious and subconscious
conclusions will change according to revealed truth.

The Process of Personal Inner Healing

During inner healing, different formats are followed that bring varying degrees of freedom to an individual's life. God, however, is not limited to any system we devise. He is omnipotent and omnipresent. He can heal however and wherever he chooses. What he does require is our agreement, which allows him to heal our wounds.[2]

We are born into a sinful world and have less-than-perfect families. However loving and caring—or unloving and uncaring—our families, the inevitable dysfunctions affect every member. Due to our own sinfulness, our reactions to these dysfunctions make matters worse. Sometimes in ignorance, and often subconsciously, we try to escape the pain of our pasts through coping and defense mechanisms, codependent relationships, and addictions. These only compound our problems. We feel hurt, rejected, resentful, and anxious. We perpetuate what we have learned and internalize what we believe to be true, even though our perceptions of truth are distorted by our own self-centered belief systems and our selfish, subjective views.

We also have an enemy who is a liar, a deceiver, and a destroyer. Jesus said the devil is a thief who has come to steal, kill, and destroy; but he (Jesus) wants us to have an abundant life.[3] The word "abundant" means *more than is necessary, surpassing, extraordinary*, and *more excellent*.

Inner healing works because it heals us from the inside out, freeing us from bondage to the past. It changes our faulty belief systems and our negative core perspectives concerning our relationships. After the pain from past memories has been healed, our lives change and we can
- set healthy boundaries;
- see life, other people, God, and ourselves in a positive light;
- let go of the past;
- give up not only the need to control other people and circumstances but also the accompanying worry.

In addition, we no longer see ourselves as victims and can make positive, healthy, and sound decisions. Unfortunately, many Christians feel inner healing is a new-age ritual. Before going any further, we want to dispel this myth.

Visualization

Inner healing is *not* visualization, but it does involve our minds recalling particular memories. Those who regard it as such may have been victimized by someone who manipulated the process, creating a "counterfeit" form of visualization. Such people "persuade, insinuate, direct," or use other tactics to create false images in a person's mind. These people perform a great injustice. This is

> *We cannot conjure Jesus up as if he were a genie in a bottle, nor will he barge into a memory without being invited.*

akin to witchcraft. In our ministry, the person being prayed for is asked to invite Jesus to come into the actual memory—what the person sees in their mind's eye, the actual traumatic situation or experience.

It is scriptural to see or hear Jesus in our mind's eyes. Daniel was lying on his bed caught up in a dream and vision when he saw Jesus.[4] Paul heard Jesus' voice.[5] The Lord called to Ananias in a vision.[6] Peter heard and answered the Lord in a vision.[7] John received the book of Revelation, and saw and heard the Lord in a vision.

Control

As prayer counselors, we must remember that we are *not* controlling the process. We are facilitators, asking specific questions relating to the memories being worked through. We intercede for a counselee as he or she works through specific beliefs and feelings.

The Holy Spirit has complete control over the process with agreement from the one being prayed for. Questions, not directives, are what we use to help guide the session.

Testimony

"My marriage is stronger and better. The peace in our household after so many years is priceless. We forgive more easily and don't hold grudges."

Discernment

As prayer counselors, we may be given discernment from the Holy Spirit concerning a specific issue a counselee is dealing with. For instance, he may reveal a soul tie, a curse, or a bitter root judgment. We can then lead the counselee through a prayer to break these issues or ask the person to pray without guidance. But if we receive discernment into a specific memory, we must reframe what is discerned in the form of a question.

For example, Mike, a fifty-two-year-old father of three, came to me (Dr. Jerry) for counsel over difficulty in communicating with his wife. While we were going through an inner healing session together, the Holy Spirit showed Mike a memory of his family gathering in their apartment's kitchen. Part of this memory involved a stairway. It was pitch black. Mike was not sure what this meant, but I knew in my spirit that it represented something he associated with his father and something he feared.

I asked him, "Would you be willing to ask the Holy Spirit to show you why the stairway is so black?"

Mike did so and immediately realized he was afraid of the blackness because his father used this same stairway every time he entered their apartment in a drunken stupor. The blackness represented hopelessness and despair. As soon as he heard his father coming up the stairs, Mike knew he was in for a beating. Even though I was given discernment about the stairway, it was not my place to insinuate or say directly what I felt. My job was to ask questions and intercede. The Holy Spirit was quite capable of giving Mike the insight he needed.

Is there ever a place where we can tell a counselee what we have discerned? Yes—as confirmation to the counselee, *after* the memory has been prayed through and we are discussing the events.

A Single Session

Inner healing is not a cure-all, nor is it a one-time prayer session. As with most counseling, inner healing is most effective when done in several sessions over time. We have often seen the Holy Spirit bring an individual back to the same memory many times in order to deal with issues that affect the person's current life.

In Mike's case, he was continually abused sexually as a child. On one particular day, more than one family member molested him. Even though he had dealt with this memory in previous inner healing sessions, he felt we needed to revisit it. He felt it related to difficulty he had in developing emotional intimacy with his wife.

During our prayer session, Mike remembered the first time he was abused on that particular day. He recalled he cried out for help, but no one can to rescue him. His parents weren't home. Feelings and thoughts of abandonment, rejection, worthlessness, and isolation flooded his mind. He realized he had vowed to never ask for help from anyone again. They wouldn't hear his cry. This inner vow had affected his ability to "open up" to his wife.

We are often asked, "Why won't God heal me from all of my past hurts at one time?" There are several reasons for this:

- Instinct. God knows what we can handle. Inner healing is similar to having emotional surgery. Just as multiple surgeries cannot be performed on our physical body at one time, neither can multiple inner healings. We will instinctively know how much we want to deal with at one time. It is important to be sensitive to our own needs. In between prayer sessions, the Holy Spirit will bring further understanding and healing. Progressively, we will sense inner changes that affect our outward lives. Jesus said that the truth will *make* us free.[8] This involves a process over time.

- Reliance on God. If God were to set us free from everything at once, we would lose our reliance on him. Working through inner healing issues over time teaches us to wait on God and his timing. We all want instant fixes, but God has a bigger picture in mind for our lives than we do. We can see the past and the present, but he sees our futures as well.

- Increase in faith. Miraculous healings do little to strengthen our faith over the long haul. We often have a "What have you done for me lately?" mentality toward God. Healing our memories over time is akin to following an exercise program; it takes time to reach the level of health we want to achieve.

Through experience, we have developed a time-tested, step-by-step approach to inner healing. As you read through it, our prayer for you is that "the very God of peace sanctify you through and through; and your whole spirit and soul and body be preserved blameless unto the coming of our Lord Jesus Christ" (1 Thessalonians 5:23).

Step by Step

At *Evangel*, the church we oversee, we host inner healing and deliverance seminars. It is open to all, and hundreds of written testimonies attest to the freedom received through inner healing. We also have a limited number of ministers available to counsel one-on-one. Because we have developed a time-tested procedure, we do not feel it is necessary to send ministers through weeks of training before they are ready for ministry. Each minister receives an easy-to-follow *Minister's Advanced Inner Healing Tips Sheet* containing the following outline:

1. Ask the counselee, "Are you willing to let Jesus take you by the hand and walk you through some memories to bring healing today?"

2. Ask the counselee to close his or her eyes, then pray over him or her: "Jesus, I thank you for _____. He/she is willing and desires to be set free from the lies and deception of the enemy today. I thank you that you are here with us and you have promised to never leave us or forsake us. I bind _____'s mind to the mind of Jesus Christ. In Jesus' name, I take authority over all the demonic forces trying to hinder or bring blockage or confusion during this time of healing. I speak to every evil spirit and I command you to be silent and step aside. Jesus, I ask that you would begin to stir up those emotions and memories that you want to bring to _____ in order to see him/her healed and set free in Jesus' name."

3. Begin by asking a question such as, "What is your most pressing need or hurt? What feelings do you struggle with the most? What issue would you like to deal with first?"

4. The counselee says, "Jesus, take me to the memory you want me to go to."

5. Ask, "What comes up right now in your memory? What happened in that situation and how old were you?" Then allow the person to share whatever details he or she wishes.

6. Ask, "How did this incident make you feel, and what emotion is the most intense?" Record all feelings shared.

7. Ask the counselee to embrace the most intense emotion(s) he or she was feeling and have him or her say, "Jesus, take me back to the root of where these feelings are coming from."

8. Record the memory or memories, and repeat steps four and five until God shows the counselee that he or she has arrived at the memory containing the original source of his or her pain.

9. Address any bitter root judgments, curses, soul ties, and unforgiveness toward others, God, and self. Ask the counselee to renounce each spirit one at a time (we have found that a spirit can disguise itself as a feeling, thus any feeling could also be a spirit). Ask the counselee to release the person that wounded him or her, as well as himself or herself, from each of these.

10. The counselee asks, "Jesus, what do you want to show me? What was the lie that I believed in this memory? Jesus, what is your truth?" Record what the person shares.

11. The counselee asks, "Jesus is there anything else I need to know about this memory?" Briefly record what is said.

12. Ask the counselee to invite Jesus into the memory. What is he doing, or what is he showing the counselee? Then ask, "Is there any more associated pain?" (At this point, because Jesus has revealed truth to the person, and because the person has seen, sensed, felt, or touched Jesus in his or her memory, he or she usually feels little or no emotional pain.)

13. If the intense negative emotions are no longer present, ask the counselee to go back through the previously listed memories from step eight, and record how true those same emotions feel to him or her now. Repeat the above steps for each memory as necessary.

14. If the emotions are gone, seal each memory in the blood of Jesus and pray a prayer of affirmation over the counselee. Afterward, the counselee will still have the memory, but the hurt and pain

should no longer be present. The counselee's wounded spirit has been healed.

Testimony

"The teaching was interesting and biblically sound.
The hands-on ministry to train in-house ministers was
presented with humility and power."

Specific Guidelines

There are specific guidelines we use during an inner healing session. We have also trained our ministry team to use these. However, before any ministry takes place—either one-on-one or in our seminar—we clearly state that our ministry team members are not professional counselors. They are volunteer prayer ministers. Each person seeking ministry must sign a legal waiver stating he or she is doing so by his or her own free will and feels that God has directed him or her. This helps to protect the ministry team and the person seeking ministry.

During our monthly seminar, each person goes through inner healing before deliverance. When the roots are removed, demons can then be renounced and removed more easily. Here is a breakdown of the guidelines we use:

1. *Are you willing?* The counselee must be in agreement for any inner healing to take place.[9] Any reluctance will hinder the counselee from receiving the healing he or she desires. The prayer minister anoints the counselee with oil, then leads him or her in prayer, asking the Holy Spirit to take control of the session and direct the counselee to specific memories.

2. *Closed eyes.* The counselee is asked to keep his or her eyes closed throughout the inner healing session except for agreed upon breaks. Doing so eliminates outside distractions and helps the counselee concentrate on the memory the Holy Spirit brings to mind.

3. *What is God showing you?* The Holy Spirit knows what memories are holding the counselee in bondage and in what order he wishes to deal with them. He is in control of the entire process.
4. *How old are you?* Jesus asked this same question.[10] It is important to know the counselee's age (at the time of the event brought to mind by the Holy Spirit) because the earlier in life the memory occurs, the greater the chance of reaching the true root of woundedness.
5. *Where were you, what happened, and who was involved?* This allows the counselee to feel what he or she felt at the time the event took place. It is important to remind the counselee *not* to see the memory objectively—i.e. through his or her current age. For example, if a memory occurred at age seven, the person should try to feel what he or she felt as a seven-year-old. The person may have to be reminded to "stay in the memory" and not see it from an adult perspective. Doing so draws out the counselee's true feelings.
6. *How did it make you feel?* Feelings are experiential, meaning that a counselee views his or her feelings as subjective truth. "If I feel something, then it has to be true." Feelings govern actions and reactions. It is important for the counselee to try to feel the emotions within a particular memory so God can provide freedom from the associated pain. Note: The prayer counselor does not determine whether or not a memory is true. If the memory *feels* true to the counselee, then that is what matters.)
7. *Renounce feelings that could be spirits.* Demonic spirits often have the same names as those of the counselee's feelings. For example, if someone feels fearful, there may be a spirit of fear behind the emotion.[11] When the counselee renounces a spirit, the person is casting it out of his or her life and forbidding it to influence him or her anymore.
8. *Forgive all involved, including God and yourself.* Forgiveness is foundational to a counselee's freedom. If the person cannot forgive, it is important to find out why and address his or her issues and concerns. The counselee cannot be manipulated into forgiv-

ing others. Jesus does not work this way. Instead, the person must forgive according to his or her own volition.

9. *Address specifics*. The prayer counselor asks the counselee to break any generational curses, word curses, soul ties, bitter root judgments, inner vows, and agreements the Holy Spirit reveals.

10. Ask Jesus: *"What is the lie I believed?"* The lie embedded in the memory has become the truth the counselee believes today, such as "I'm unloved; I'm stupid; I can't do anything right; it's all my fault." The source of the emotional pain can be traced to a specific lie or lies the person believed when the incident took place. It *may* have been implanted in the mind by a demon. Because it was accepted as truth, the lie gives a demon legal access to the person's life. It is an integral part of the counselee's belief system and is one of many roots influencing his or her current thoughts, behavior, actions, and reactions.

11. Ask Jesus: *"What is your truth?"* The truth Jesus speaks to the counselee sets him or her free of the pain associated with a particular memory. It replaces the lie the counselee believed was true.

12. *Invite Jesus into the memory*. Jesus will not violate a counselee's free will; he is a gentleman. The prayer counselor asks the counselee, "Would you like to invite Jesus into the memory?" The person is reassured that Jesus will never leave or forsake him or her. If the counselee agrees, Jesus will be visible in whatever way best meets the counselee's need. If the person does not want to invite Jesus into the memory, the prayer counselor now has another avenue to explore with further questions.

13. *What is Jesus doing?* Jesus will act, speak, or reveal himself in a meaningful way to the counselee. The prayer counselor asks the counselee what Jesus is doing and rejoices with the counselee.

14. *Rating the memory*. After the counselee has worked through the memory, the prayer counselor asks him or her to scan the memory. If the counselee still feels painful emotions associated with the memory, he or she can decide if it is worth exploring this memory for further roots and lies.

15. *Seal with the blood and prayer of affirmation.* We seal the time of prayer with the blood of Jesus for protection. The counselee then thanks Jesus for revealing truth about the memory. The revealed truth now becomes part of his or her belief system.

Testimony

"I never realized I was carrying around
so much junk inside of me.
What a shame to have not realized how
much healing I needed.
I thank God for the sacrifices and obedience of the
ministers; I was set free from cigarettes."

Final Note

Inner healing is a *process* of spiritual, relational, and emotional restoration under the guidance of the Holy Spirit. The healing received allows us to make better choices and decisions because we are no longer influenced by pain from the past. The counselee should be encouraged to go through future inner healing sessions, allowing for time in between each one.

God's desire is to restore our spirits and souls whenever we invite Jesus into our emotional wounds. After receiving healing, we can see and accept the truth about our pasts, we can function more effectively in our current circumstances and relationships, and we're able to see brighter futures.

Testimony

"I was set free from a 16-year addiction to laxatives.
I realize I must now work on mindsets to get
completely free."

Chapter 9 The Process of Personal Inner Healing

1 – Matthew 7:19- 20
2 – Amos 3:3
3 – John 10:10
4 – Daniel 7:1, 13
5 – Acts 9:4
6 – Acts 9:10
7 – Acts 10:9-16
8 – John 8:32
9 – Amos 3:3
10 – Mark 9:21
11 – 2 Timothy 1:7

CHAPTER 10

Deliverance

Throughout our twenty-five years in deliverance, we have seen thousands of people set free from the oppression and influence of demons. We have also witnessed yokes, strongholds, bondages, curses, soul ties, and more removed from their lives. People with anger issues have been freed, those bound to addictions have been loosed, and habitual strongholds—such as obsessive-compulsive behaviors—have been broken.

Many Christians and Christian leaders do not believe in or accept deliverance as a biblical mandate for the Church. We hope the following chapters will dispel any myths and erroneous teachings about deliverance ministries.

Testimony

After going through deliverance at another ministry, I thought we had covered all the areas. But I got massively set free and now notice a tremendous difference."

The Ministry of Deliverance

In its simplest form, deliverance is appropriating the finished work of Christ on Calvary. Deliverance is the casting out of demonic influence and/or oppression from a person's life by the authority of Jesus' name and through his blood. Jesus and his disciples performed deliverance on Jews and non-Jews alike. The ministries of deliverance and inner healing together remove the "kinks and creases" in our spiritual armor caused by our own woundedness. These wounds are the grounds that give demonic forces the legal right to enter our lives and influence, harass, and oppress us.

The ministry of deliverance is not listed in five-fold ministry gifts of Ephesians 4 because it is a *body* ministry. It is not limited to a select group of ministers. All Christians are called to participate in deliverance ministry, but only those who step out in faith will answer the call.[1]

The New Testament is full of deliverance examples. Jesus gave the seventy power over the enemy.[2] They came back rejoicing, saying, "Lord, even the demons submit to us in your name."[3] Jesus charged his disciples—and us—with the Great Commission, giving us power to cast out demons.[4] Jesus stated that he had been given all power in heaven and earth, which he then passed on to his disciples and to us today.[5]

In our opinion, a ministry of deliverance should be part of the fabric of the local church just like praise and worship, preaching, and teaching. But it *must* be anchored in the Word of God—not in experience alone. Sadly, it is often maligned due to comparisons with made-for-movie exorcisms, incorrect theology, fear of demonic attacks, fear of loss of support, fear of loss of church membership, fear of loss of personal reputation, and even fear of losing one's salvation.

Incorrect Theology

When discussing deliverance ministry, we often encounter people who argue against it by quoting one or two Scriptures. The most common ones are 2 Peter 2:10-11 and Jude 8-9. In these Scriptures, the words "slander" and "slanderous" are used, which mean *a false and unfounded accusation*. As believers, we do not bring slanderous accusations against demons. Our warfare is based on the truth of God's Word and our authority in Jesus Christ. In Jude, Michael used the name of the Lord to rebuke Satan (verse 9). Our authority comes from the Name above all Names—Jesus Christ. Through him we can resist and rebuke the enemy.[6]

Many believers feel that because Jesus defeated Satan at Calvary there is no more warfare. They state that demons cannot attack Christians. However, in the New Testament, Paul and the other disciples referred to and experienced spiritual warfare on various levels. Their lives and the books they wrote prove that spiritual warfare continues today. For instance, the apostles performed miraculous signs and wonders among the people, including healing those tormented by evil spirits.[7] Philip drove out evil spirits and healed paralytics and cripples.[8] Among the deliverances Paul performed, one involved driving out a spirit of divination from a slave girl.[9] In Acts 19, seven sons of Sceva tried to drive out evil spirits using the name of Jesus.[10] However, the demon did not recognize their authority—but it certainly knew who Jesus and Paul were. Our point is that the book of Acts was written *after* Jesus' resurrection, and warfare continued.

Fear

Whether through leadership or the congregation, fear is a huge deterrent to participation in deliverance ministry. Deliverance is trench warfare. The enemy does not fight fair, and people are often afraid of what will come their way in retaliation. Ministry leaders are afraid of losing church members, financial support, or church and personal reputation. Due to a lack of education and teaching, a congregation may oppose any aspect of deliverance. Individuals may have seen or gone through a deliverance session but, because it was not biblically balanced (i.e. not everything is a demon) and produced little freedom, these people want nothing more to do with deliverance ministry.

The Bible is clear that fear is a spirit and that this spirit is not from God.[11] The enemy causes us to be fearful through lies, deception, and ignorance. Fear is no reason to shy away from deliverance. In Jesus' words,

"These things I have spoken unto you, that in me ye might have peace. In the world ye shall have tribulation: but be of good cheer; I have overcome the world" (John 16:33).

> *Deliverance is trench warfare.*

Sometimes a minister will promise that everything is going to be fixed in a person's life after he or she receives deliverance. When this doesn't happen, people become discouraged and lose hope. We state unequivocally: Deliverance is not a cure-all. Both inner healing and deliverance are tools used by God as part of a believer's process of sanctification. As long as we live in this world and battle our flesh, we will be exposed to sin, we will sin, and we will come under attack. Biblically balanced inner healing and deliverance go hand-in-hand with Bible-based counseling.

An effective deliverance ministry includes
1. pastoral covering and involvement;
2. sound teaching;
3. accountability and submission;
4. training and activation;
5. a safe environment;
6. preparation on the part of the one receiving deliverance;
7. follow-up;
8. prayer and fasting.

Fortunately, deliverance ministries are springing up throughout the nation as thousands of pastors realize there is demonic bondage within their congregations, their own lives, and the lives of their family members. We commend all who are participating in this ministry and pray that God continues to give revelation, wisdom, and guidance, as well as victory over all of the works of the devil. We encourage all ministers who are not sure about this vital ministry to seek out those who are experienced.

Testimony

"Your teams who ministered with me during the
deliverance sessions were good workers
and took authority in the Spirit; they were persistent!"

Exorcism

If you've watched or heard about a movie that depicts an exorcism, you may have noticed that only "men of the cloth" who carry a cross perform them. These people invoke chants and scream at the devil trying to get results. In the meantime, the one who is "possessed" strikes fear and terror into the hearts of those around them, including the minister. The thought of exorcism (an extreme form of deliverance) conjures up all kinds of blood-curdling images and spooky images in our minds. Rarely do these happen. The people in such movies do not know their authority in Christ, similar to the seven sons of Sceva.

When Jesus addressed a demon, he had authority over it, and the demon knew this to be true.[12] He did not scream, rant, and rave trying to drive a demon out. He simply commanded the unclean spirit to leave, and it obeyed. As believers in Christ, we have Jesus' authority as well.

We are seated with Christ "far above all principality, and power, and might, and dominion, and every name that is named, not only in this world, but also in that which is to come" (Ephesians 1:21).

It is his name and authority that we use against the enemy in deliverance ministry. However, demons do not always come out the first time they are commanded to do so. In Mark 5:8, Jesus confronted an unclean spirit and commanded it to come out of the man in whom it dwelled. (Note: The wording, "Come out of the man," is a direct quote from Jesus.) If the spirit had immediately obeyed its Creator, who had all power and authority, verses 9-12 would not have been written. In verse 13 we realize the demon did obey. However, our point is that the demon initially resisted Jesus' direct command. If it resisted Jesus' authority, could it resist ours as well? Also, it is possible that Jesus allowed a level of demonic resistance so that the tormented man could partake in his own deliverance—giving him time to agree and send the spirit packing. That would ensure that the person would want to *remain* free.

In many places in the New Testament, the word "word" can be translated *conversation* when used in spiritual warfare terminology, meaning more than one spoken word. There are times when a demon must be commanded to come out more than once before it gives up its habitation.

In the gospels, Jesus was attacked by the devil through temptation in the wilderness. He rebuked Satan three times using the Word of God before the devil finally left him for a season. In Ephesians 6:12, Paul states that we *wrestle* against demonic entities. In 2 Corinthians 10:3-5, he says that we pull down strongholds. Wrestling and pulling down mean we exert energy in spiritual warfare. There are a number of factors that determine how quickly a demon will respond to our command, such as

- its demonic strength based on the foothold it has established;
- a person holding unforgiveness;
- whether the demon is inside or outside;
- its assignment.

There are times when we must repetitively and authoritatively command demons to release their holds on a person's life. At other times, it is simply a one-time rebuke.

Possession Versus Oppression

"If the Holy Spirit resides within a Christian, how can he or she be totally possessed by a demon?" Dr. Sherill and I are asked this question all the time.

There are some Christians who say, "I am born again, a new creature in Christ; and light, not darkness dwells in me." These are correct statements in regard to our *reborn spirit*. The enemy cannot *totally possess* our spirits, because the Holy Spirit dwells there. However, evil spirits and demons can dwell in our souls and bodies. These are unregenerate areas that need to go through the process of sanctification. It is through them that the enemy gains a legal right to attack and oppress us.

There are also Christians who believe people can have demons in their spirits. They quote King David, who asked God to create a clean and upright spirit within him. [13] They also quote the following verse:

"Having therefore these promises, dearly beloved, let us cleanse ourselves from all filthiness of the flesh and spirit, perfecting holiness in the fear of God" (2 Corinthians 7:1).

The word "filthiness" means *defilement or actions that bring defilement*. In this verse, "flesh" refers to the body. "Spirit" can mean both soul and spirit, including our life force.

Those who believe we can have demons in our spirits refer to the fact that Satan himself entered into Judas.[14] Practical experience also points out that when demons are cast out of a person, there is agitation in the person's stomach area—the same place a person's spirit is thought to reside.

We believe that Christians cannot be *completely possessed* by demonic spirits because the Holy Spirit dwells in us. Possession implies ownership. But we can "have demons." We can be oppressed, harassed, or influenced within our soul realms; and our spirits can become contaminated by demonic forces.

Variations of the word *possess* occur more than twenty-six times in the New Testament and hundreds of times in the Old Testament. From the outset of his ministry, Jesus delivered untold numbers of people who were possessed by devils.[15] The word "possess" means *to be under the power of a demon; to be afflicted with severe diseases, either bodily or mentally; to express the mind and consciousness of indwelling demons; to be vexed or have a devil.* In our modern-day understanding of demonic possession, we refer to movies such as *The Exorcist* or *Rosemary's Baby.* These movies depict demons as having total control and dominion, and therefore possession, of a person. However, in the Greek, the word possession does not mean total ownership or rulership. It means to be demonized or to have a demon(s). These are two completely different concepts.

In the Bible, the nation of Israel can be compared to the Body of Christ collectively and to Christians individually. However, there are two distinctions that must be made: First, both Israelites and Christians are heirs of salvation. However, the Old Testament Israelites were not possessors of it—they were not born-again believers. They believed in God and followed his ways but were not indwelt by the Holy Spirit. Second, the Israelites and Christians are both under blood covenant. The nation of Israel was under one made through the blood of animals, while a Christian's covenant is based on the blood of Christ. The Bible states the New Testament covenant is a far superior one, based on better promises, that speaks of better things than the blood of animals.[16]

The question must be asked, "Who did Jesus cast devils out of most often?" He cast them out of the Israelites—God's covenant children, the apple of his eye, and his special chosen race! A demon could possess an Israelite, but it cannot totally possess a born-again believer who is sealed with the Holy Spirit (see Ephesians 1:13; 4:30).

Jesus was very clear that deliverance was part of an Israelite's inheritance. He called it *the children's bread.*

> For a certain woman, whose young daughter had an unclean spirit, heard of him, and came and fell at his feet: The woman was a Greek, a Syrophenician by nation; and she besought him that he would cast forth the devil out of her daughter. But Jesus said unto her, Let the children first be filled: for it is not meet to take the children's bread, and to cast it unto the dogs. And she answered and said unto him, Yes, Lord: yet the dogs under the table eat of the children's crumbs. And he said unto her, For this saying go thy way; the devil is gone out of thy daughter. And when she was come to her house, she found the devil gone out, and her daughter laid upon the bed.
>
> Mark 7:25-30

Herein we see deliverance by proxy. The mother had faith in Jesus' ability to deliver her daughter, and she interceded for her. Jesus recognized her faith, even though she was Greek, and rewarded her. However, he also said that driving demons out (deliverance) was the children's bread, meaning it primarily belonged to the children of Israel.

> And, behold, there was a woman which had a spirit of infirmity eighteen years, and was bowed together, and could in no wise lift up herself. And when Jesus saw her, he called her to him, and said unto her, Woman, thou art loosed from thine infirmity. And he laid his hands on her: and immediately she was made straight, and glorified God. ... And ought not this woman, being a daughter of Abraham, whom Satan hath bound, lo, these eighteen years, be loosed from this bond on the sabbath day?
>
> Luke 13:11-13, 16

In this passage, the word infirmity means *a sickness or disease or weakness.* The vast majority of deliverances performed by Jesus centered on the Israelites. However, as the above verses prove, it was not exclusive to the Israelite nation. Nor were his deliverances

120

limited to a particular setting or region. He cast demons out of people mainly in synagogues but also in villages, in cities, in the country-side, and at the seaside; he cast out demons outside of Simon Peter's mother-in-law's house; he cast out demons in person and from a dis-tance. Deliverance was an integral part of Jesus' everyday ministry. Some people he touched, for others he commanded demons to come straight out. He asked some demons their names; others he com-manded to be silent. As Sovereign Lord with authority over the entire demonic kingdom, Jesus delivered those who came to him in what-ever manner he chose.

This tells us there are many ways to deliver people from demonic spirits. Those in deliverance ministry who believe their way is the model to follow—because of the fruit of changed lives from their ministry—should take note of Jesus' methodology and not condemn those who have different methods or venues. No one ministry has all the answers. God uses different ways and different methods at different times to deliver his people as he chooses. We can learn from each other and should not isolate ourselves from other ministries.

The Body of Christ has been spiritually engrafted into the Israelite nation, and we are joint heirs to all the blessings and promises of God—including deliverance. Thus, deliverance is truly the children's bread; it is predominately for born-again believers in every denomination, in every community, and in every nation.

Believers cannot be completely possessed by demons; but we can be oppressed, attacked, harassed, or influenced by one or more. How is this possible?

The New Testament Greek word for "spirit" is *pneuma*. The New Testament Greek word for "soul" is *psyche*. When we are born again, the Holy Spirit brings to life, fills, and communes with our spirit. He gives us God's life, and our spirit is completely under his control.[17] Our flesh, however, is not under the Spirit's control. On the contrary, it wars against the Spirit.[18] It is our flesh—our body, soul, mind, will, and emo-tions—in which demons look to gain legal footholds in our lives. Once they have established legal entry, demons look to expand their territory within us through yokes, bondages, and strongholds in order to dictate to and control us.

As born-again believers, we are responsible for keeping our lives free from the enemy's influence through the power of the Holy Spirit. Jesus said, "For the prince of this world cometh, and hath nothing in me."[19] The Bible states that we are to crucify our flesh; die to self; do all things without murmuring and complaining; rid ourselves of things such as malice, anger, discord, and strife; submit to God; *and* resist the devil. As we learn to do these things and appropriate our faith and position in Christ, demonic spirits will have fewer areas of influence in our lives.

Paul wrote, "Holding faith, and a good conscience; which some having put away concerning faith have made shipwreck; of whom is Hymenaeus and Alexander, whom I have delivered unto Satan, that they may learn not to blaspheme" (1 Timothy 1:19-20).

He also stated, "In meekness instructing those that oppose themselves; if God peradventure will give them repentance to the acknowledging of the truth; And that they may recover themselves out of the snare of the devil, who are taken captive by him at his will" (2 Timothy 2:25-26).

However, we have all sinned and fallen short of God's glory and his perfection.[20] Thus God has given the Body of Christ the ministry of deliverance to free ourselves (through the power of the Holy Spirit) from the enemy's grip. Jesus came to destroy *all* of the devil's works, and indeed he did.[21] He also said that he will build his church, and the gates of hell will not prevail against it.[22] The Body of Christ is the Church, and Jesus has given us his power to cast out the enemy through deliverance.

Demonic Influence

We have often been asked, "How do demonic spirits enter into a person's life?"

They do so through legal footholds and open doors created when we violate God's laws. Just as there are consequences in the natural world when we resist or violate natural principles, there are consequences when we break spiritual laws. For instance, if I were to jump off a building hoping to fly, the law of gravity would pull me to earth and painfully remind me that I am not designed that way. In the spiritual realm, when I break the law of forgiveness by holding a grudge or not forgiving some-one, it gives a spirit the legal right to torment me.

Demonic spirits may enter a person's life in several ways:

- Conception: A baby that was born out of wedlock, was given up for adoption, or has an absentee father might suffer from rejection, from being ignored, or from fear of abandonment.
- Sin: Whenever we sin, we give the enemy a legal entry into our lives.
- Generational curses/assignments: Deuteronomy 28, Numbers 14:18, and Jeremiah 14:20 are good examples.
- Detestable objects in our possession: In 1 Kings 11, King Solomon's heart was turned away from God by his many wives and concubines. Among his sins, he kept foreign idols and built high places for them to be worshipped.
- Ungodly soul ties
- Inner vows and bitter root judgments
- Doubt and unbelief
- Traumatic experiences
- Unforgiveness, bitterness, and resentment

Manifestations

When Jesus rebuked or cast out a demon, often there were manifestations. Sometimes Jesus would forbid a demon to talk when casting it out. Other times the demon would come out with a shriek, a loud voice, or a cry. There was often a convulsion or foaming at the mouth. We have seen these types of displays.

A good example is the man who brought his son to Jesus.[23] The son had a dumb spirit. The spirit often seized the boy, throwing him to the ground. Upon seeing Jesus, the spirit threw the boy into a convulsion, and he rolled around while foaming at the mouth. Seven verses later, Jesus rebuked the spirit, and it "rent him sore and came out of him." Jesus let the spirit manifest while he talked to the father about its entry (dealing with the root from childhood). There are times in deliverance sessions that a demon will manifest before releasing its hold on a person.

The word "rent" means to convulse with a spasmodic contraction." It is the Greek root for the modern-day word "epilepsy."

"For unclean spirits, crying with loud voice, came out of many that were possessed with them: and many taken with palsies, and that were lame, were healed" (Acts 8:7).

Some people scoff and say there is no need for a spirit to manifest at all. There are times this is true. Manifestations are not always needed to indicate freedom from a demon. However, when Jesus cast out a demon—unless he specifically told it to be quiet—there were times when a demon would physically manifest before leaving its host. Why would this be any different today?

Jesus also stated there were "certain kinds" of spirits that could be cast out only by prayer *and* fasting.[24] There are times when—no matter how many people gather to pray in agreement and intercession; to use the principles of binding and loosing and spiritual warfare; to plead the blood; to use praise and worship as a weapon of war; or to use banners, flags, and dance against the enemy—unless these same people *fast*, a demon can maintain its position within its host.

In our seminars, we have seen people cry, shout, scream, cough, yawn, sneeze, and exhibit other such manifestations. We have come to accept these as normal. Our seminar attendees are told that, whenever they feel agitated, relief is spelled s-c-r-e-a-m. However, we do not allow demons to manifest in ways that draw attention to themselves, such as causing someone to slither like a snake or howl like a dog. We take authority over the spirit and bind it (forbid it to manifest in these ways). A demon must come out in decency and order, and in a manner that is compliant to Scripture. Deliverance ministry should *always* bring honor and glory to God, and *never* to a demonic spirit.

Naming a Spirit

There are many good books written on the hierarchy of Satan's kingdom, and it is good for all deliverance ministers to be aware of the adversary. Just like in battles fought on this earth, knowing how one's enemy works is a key to victory. However, in a deliverance session, it is not as important to name specific demons by their names as it is to call them out by how they operate. For example, a spirit of fear can take on a number of guises, such as anxiety, worry, or panic. A spirit of infirmity can attack the spirit, soul, and body. It should be noted that of the thirty-nine times God dealt with spirits in the Bible, only once did Jesus specifically ask its name.[25]

Deliverance ministers who engage demons in conversation can become sidetracked. A demon's native language is lying. There is no reason to engage it in conversation to obtain its name, its legal access into a person's life, or for any other information. Demons are simply to be cast out. It is more important for a minister to hear the voice of the Holy Spirit rather than try to extract information from a lying demon.

Methods of Deliverance

In and of themselves, those who perform deliverance have no authority over demonic forces. However, as born-again believers we have Jesus Christ's authority over all demonic forces. We use
- the name of Jesus;[26]
- the Word;[27]
- the blood of Jesus[28] for remission of sins,[29] atonement,[30] justification,[31] redemption,[32] and peace;[33]
- binding and loosing. [34]

Jesus "cast out" the money changers, stating that they had made his Father's house (the Temple) a den of thieves.[35] The phrase "cast out"—used more than one hundred fifty times throughout the Bible—means *to drive out, to drive away, to thrust away, to draw out with force, to tear out*, particularly in the New Testament when referring to demons. When Jesus compared the moneychangers to thieves, he used the same word he used in John 10:10 in describing the thief as one who has come "to steal, and to kill, and to destroy." Those who believe in deliverance have the authority to "cast out" demons from another believer because the demons are trying to steal, kill, and destroy the believer's life.

Receiving Deliverance

We do not have to fear the enemy, his tactics, or his influence. However, we live in a sinful world, full of sinful people, and we have a sinful nature. As long as we are in this world, the enemy's continual onslaught against us will affect our lives. Receiving deliverance from a biblically balanced ministry is a good way of getting rid of the contamination we pick up in this world. Dr. Sherill and I, and our family, go through deliverance once a year because of the constant attacks we face. We believe we should be submitted to that which we believe and minister in.

It is not hard to receive deliverance. First of all you must recognize your need for it. Be sure to pray and receive direction from God the best you know how before receiving deliverance.

- Do you have persistent and problematic habits and patterns in your life?
- Are there generational and hereditary issues you would like to deal with?
- Do you struggle in areas that you feel cannot be overcome by counseling alone?

Next, research various deliverance ministries until you find one you are comfortable with. Once you have made an appointment or signed up for a seminar such as the one at our church, be open to whatever God wants to do in your life, including being willing to forgive whomever God asks you to. After the deliverance session, be sure to saturate yourself and your household with the Word, worship, and prayer.

In our follow-up teaching after our seminars, we ask all attendees to spend one hour and fifteen minutes per day praying, reading, and worshipping God (this time can be broken up into manageable time slots), as well as attend church regularly, for forty consecutive days. We call this "filling the house," based on Matthew 12:43-45.

We hope that you are now comfortable with the ministry of deliverance. We do not advocate seeing demons everywhere, nor do we believe that demons are to blame for everything that goes wrong in a person's life. However, the influence of demons in a believer's life cannot be ignored.

Testimony

Delivered from Garbage

I wish to thank the Lord Jesus Christ for leading me to workshop. Through divine guidance and many unusual circumstances, Jesus led me to my appointed time with this anointed ministry. Let me first say that before going through the inner healing & deliverance seminar, I had a heart after the Lord Jesus. I was in His Word daily, was a true prayer warrior, and had a healthy communion with my Father. But I knew that somehow there were many things keeping me from the walk that God had intended for me. Through the inner healing & deliverance process I saw how much guilt, unforgiveness, and pain that was still with me even though I was a child of God. The Holy Spirit showed me the root of these problems, and Jesus Christ showed me how to overcome them. Through this I was able to see how Satan had planted seeds of homosexuality and self-condemnation in me. Through the inner healing & deliverance seminar, these unclean spirits were pulled out by their roots. I was unaware that pride, rebellion, and rejection had become the sources of whom I was.

Now that these blockages and strongholds are broken, I am able to see God in a much different light. I see how much love and compassion He has for me and each and every one of His children! My communion with the Lord has become stronger and clearer. He has shown me things I could not have received before. I pray continually that He allows this ministry to press on, freeing the children of God from so much garbage in their lives. May the Lord bless pastors Jerry and Sherill Piscopo, and the loving workers of this precious inner healing & deliverance ministry! I've been preaching the Good News now for some time, but I never felt truly anointed until the Sunday following the seminar! It's a great feeling to be used by God in such a mighty way! Praise the Lord!

Deliverance Brings Freedom in Many Areas of Life

I praise the God of my salvation that he has delivered me from the hands of my enemies and from them that were too mighty for me! I feel that I have found a home here at Evangel. (For me to even say that is a victory!) Since my deliverance I am learning to seek the praise of God and not of men. Jesus has become very precious to me as I have felt his nearness, have experienced an increased awareness of spiritual battles, and have increased courage and discernment on how to fight them. I have felt a renewed desire for holiness—to make my life, home, and responses pleasing to God.

There has been a dramatically increased ability within me to take care of my responsibilities around the home without complaining, avoiding them, or putting them off. I actually desire to be responsible in these areas. I've found myself caring more about what I look like and taking more time to take care of myself. I didn't desire food just to eat it.

Things seem clearer to me now. When I'm battling a spirit, I see it as a spirit and can successfully rebuke it because of the clearer understanding I am gaining, through scripture and prayer, about the authority I have because of the blood of Jesus. It has been amazing to me how fruitful my prayer times have been. God has unfolded his wisdom to me in Scripture in a way I haven't experienced in years.

I've gained new perspectives on loving and understanding my husband. There seems to be a real difference in how I speak to my husband. The things I noticed immediately were a lack of urgency to speak and a loss of need to control, unlike I had before. I've been called on and emboldened by God to display my Christianity and not to guard my reputation. I've been able to respond graciously under pressure and actually bless those who persecute me. I've begun again to be free to use expressive dance as a form of worship.

I've noticed a real difference in how this month's menstrual cycle has been. Although I have had some unexplained tears, I haven't experienced the dramatic emotional ups and downs that normally accompany it. The pain has been normal instead of unbearable. Since the deliverance workshop I have held babies and experienced joy in doing so without tears, remorse or bitterness.

I've experienced a liberty and clarity of thought, enabling me to assess priorities. The Lord has given me compassion and the ability to forgive. It is easier to focus on salvation by grace rather than by works. Negative and critical thoughts of leaders and those in authority are not as big a problem. Thanks to all you brothers and sisters who have been willing to make so many sacrifices to help me toward this new freedom.

Chapter 10 Deliverance

1 – Mark 16:17
2 – Luke 10:10-17
3 – Luke 10:17
4 – Mark 16:15-18
5 – Matthew 18:18
6 – Luke 10:1-20;
    Acts 5:16; 8:7; 16:16-18; 19:12
7 – Acts 5:16
8 – Acts 8:4-7
9 – Acts 16:16-18
10 – Acts 19:10-17
11 – Romans 8:15;
    2 Timothy 1:7
12 – Matthew 8:28-30;
    Mark 1:27;
    Luke 4:36
13 – Psalm 51:10
14 – Luke 22:3
15 – Matthew 4:24, 8:16, 8:28;
    Mark 5:15;
    Luke 8:36
16 – Hebrews 8:6; 12:24
17 – 1 John 5:11-12
18 – Galatians 5:16-18
19 – John 14:30
20 – Romans 3:23
21 – 1 John 3:8
22 – Matthew 16:18
23 – Mark 9:17-27
24 – Mark 9:28-30
25 – Mark 5:9
26 – Mark 16:17
27 – Hebrews 4:12
28 – 1 John 1:7

29 – Matthew 26:28
30 – Romans 3:25
31 – Romans 5:9
32 – Ephesians 1:7
33 – Colossians 1:20
34 – Matthew 16:19,
    18:18; John 20:23
35 – Matthew 21:12-14

CHAPTER 11

Binding and Loosing

When Jesus gave the apostles—and by extension the Body of Christ—the power to bind and loose, he was giving to them the true authority that the religious leaders of his day claimed to possess. But what do the terms *bind* and *loose* mean? And why did the religious leaders claim to have these powers? What do these terms have to do with spiritual authority over demonic spirits and deliverance? Further, does the initiative to bind or loose begin with men or with God? Does the Church have the power to initiate action or decisions on earth that heaven is obligated to acknowledge? Or is Church authority governed by what has already been bound and loosed in heaven? We will answer these questions in the following pages.

Word Meanings

There are two passages in the New Testament that specifically address binding and loosing. These have historical, contextual, and spiritual significance for the Church and for individual believers.

"And I will give unto thee the keys of the kingdom of heaven: and whatsoever thou shalt bind on earth shall be bound in heaven: and whatsoever thou shalt loose on earth shall be loosed in heaven" (Matthew 16:19).

"Verily I say unto you, Whatsoever ye shall bind on earth shall be bound in heaven: and whatsoever ye shall loose on earth shall be loosed in heaven" (Matthew 18:18).

In the above verses the word "bind" means *to bind, tie, fasten; to bind, fasten with chains; to throw into chains; to bind or put under obligation to the law, duty, etc.; to forbid, prohibit, declare to be illicit.* The word "loose" means to:

release any person (or thing) tied or fastened; to unbind, release from bonds, [set free one who is] bound with chains (a prisoner); to discharge from prison, let go; to loosen, undo, or dissolve anything bound, tied, or compacted together; to dismiss, break up (an assembly); [to release from] laws as having a binding force; to annul, subvert; to do away with; to deprive of authority, whether by precept or act; to declare unlawful; to loose what is compacted or built together; to break up, demolish, destroy; to dissolve something coherent into parts; to destroy; to overthrow; to do away with.

Testimony

"This is the first time that I have not felt the 'baggage' of my past carried along on my back."

Historical Context

In ancient Hebrew culture, the religious leaders—the priests and Levites of Moses' time, and the Pharisees, Sadducees, and Sanhedrin of Jesus' time—had final authority over the *interpretation* of the Mosaic Law. There were approximately 613 instructions written in the Torah—the Hebrew bible—that governed daily life in Israel. (The New Testament contains about 1,030 commands to guide our walk with God.) These Old Testament laws told the Israelites *what* God expected of them but were not always clear on *how* to apply them; it was the religious leaders' responsibility to interpret what the law meant in context to their societies. Their interpretations *bound* or *prohibited* certain activities and *loosed* or *allowed* others, often involving the Sabbath. For example, the Torah forbade working on the Sabbath but did not define what specific activities constituted work. Thus, whatever the religious leaders bound, the nation was forbidden to do; whatever they loosed, the nation was permitted to do.

As time passed, the rabbinical interpretations became *teachings* on binding and loosing that grew in numbers and importance until they became more important in daily life than the Mosaic Law itself.[1] When disputes broke out over conflicting teachings, sects grew, which added more confusion. Their teachings grew into legalism and became too cumbersome for the common Israelite to bear. When Jesus came to the Israelite nation, the religious leaders bore his wrath and rebuke as indicated in Matthew 23:

> For they [the religious leaders] bind heavy burdens and grievous to be borne, and lay them on men's shoulders; but they themselves will not move them with one of their fingers (verse 4, brackets added).
>
> Woe unto you, scribes and Pharisees, hypocrites! for ye compass sea and land to make one proselyte, and when he is made, ye make him twofold more the child of hell than yourselves (verse 15).
>
> Ye serpents, ye generation of vipers, how can ye escape the damnation of hell? (verse 33).

Although the religious leaders publicly followed their own teachings, Jesus knew that privately—and in their hearts—they did not submit to the same strict code of conduct they expected the nation to follow. Their teachings were called *yokes*, which were minute interpretations of the Mosaic Law. The leaders threatened harsh penalties if the "letter of the law," or the laws' interpretation, was not followed. Under the guise of religion, they would travel far and wide to find potential disciples, even among the heathen nations. They wanted the glory of making disciples. Jesus publicly confronted the religious leaders, calling them hypocrites. He rebuked them for being children of the devil and for speaking lies, just like their father the devil.[2] He said they taught their disciples to become even more legalistic and bigoted, and twice the children of hell they were.[3] He rebuked them for driving the Israelites further into legalism and confusion, and away from a personal relationship with God.

Keys to the Kingdom

Jesus related the terms *binding* and *loosing* to having ownership to the keys of the kingdom of heaven.[4] Jesus gave these keys—which symbolize authority—to the disciples after his resurrection. He gave them the authority to bind and loose teachings concerning scriptural questions within the early Church. Jesus was giving them the same authority that the religious leaders claimed to have—the right to teach, bind, and loose what would be permitted or forbidden within the Church.

For example, in Acts 15, there was a controversy over whether or not Gentiles should be admitted into church fellowship without first being circumcised. When the church leadership convened in Jerusalem, Peter ruled that both Jews and Gentiles were heirs to God's kingdom.[5] In turn, James bound the Gentiles to the following:

> Wherefore my sentence is, that we trouble not them, which from among the Gentiles are turned to God: But that we write unto them, that they abstain from pollutions of idols, and from fornication, and from things strangled, and from blood. For Moses of old time hath in every city them that preach him, being read in the synagogues every sabbath day.
>
> Acts 15:19-21

"The keys to bind and loose" was a familiar term used in Jewish culture. It was bestowed upon religious leaders who completed and graduated from their studies in Jewish religion. Upon course completion of each particular law, a "key" or diploma was presented to each Jewish student as he progressed toward the high position of Doctor of Law. The key handed to each student had the words "receive authority to bind and to loose" inscribed on it. After mastering all of the Mosaic Law, the Doctor of Law could now say what was lawful and unlawful when interpreting the Mosaic Law, usually in reference to the moral code.

When Jesus gave the apostles the keys to bind and loose, among other things he gave them the authority to

- accomplish God's rule on earth, restricting on earth things that are bound or forbidden in heaven, and setting free or loosing that which is permitted in heaven;
- teach others based on laws, rules, and principles of the kingdom of God as taught by Jesus;
- bind and loose what is permitted or forbidden within a particular body of believers as well as within the Body of Christ as a whole.

Testimony

"I was drastically changed from the post-war syndrome that resulted from my service in Vietnam that has caused me endless pain and suffering."

Authority and Power

The disciples began to use the keys that Jesus gave them on the day of Pentecost. They started to bind and loose (forbid and permit) teachings and principles that are in operation in the kingdom of God and given to them by Jesus himself.

"Truly I tell you, whatever you forbid and declare to be improper and unlawful on earth *must be what is already forbidden* in heaven, and whatever you permit and declare proper and lawful on earth *must be what is already permitted* in heaven" (Matthew 18:18, Amplified Bible, italics added).

The believers who gathered on the day of Pentecost were the first members of the worldwide Church, the Body of Christ. Thus, believers today have this same authority as well. We are to teach, operate, and walk in the authority and power already at work in heaven. However, Jesus gave the apostles more than just his authority to teach—he also gave them his *power* over all the works of the devil—something the religious leaders never had. His power came upon the early Church on the Day of Pentecost when the believers were filled with the Holy Spirit.

> *Believers have the authority and power to loose freedom and liberty according to the already-established laws of the kingdom of God.*

When we look at the full meaning of the words *bind* and *loose*, we realize they refer to more than just forbidding and permitting certain teachings; they also include the power to break chains and bondages—deliverance terms used by Jesus. The religious leaders bound the Israelites, who are covenant children and believers in God, to "doctrines of devils"; but Jesus' teachings loosed "those who believed," setting them free. The devil bound many of the Israelites with sickness and diseases while oppressing and possessing others. Jesus had the power to loose these people from these bondages and chains, and did so for "those who believed."[6]

All of Jesus' authority and power has been given to the Church—specifically to "those who believe." We have the authority to teach, bind, and loose, and the power to defeat the kingdom of darkness through the great commission. Long ago Satan was cast out of heaven and could no longer exercise his authority and power there.[7] Just like the early Church leaders, believers today have the *authority* to bind his legalistic teachings and all teachings that are contrary to the Bible (doctrines of devils), as well as the *power* to bind all of the works of the enemy (his influence and oppression). Believers have the authority and power to loose freedom and liberty according to the already established laws of the kingdom of God.

Doctrines of Devils

Now the Spirit speaketh expressly, that in the latter times some shall depart from the faith, giving heed to seducing spirits, and doctrines of devils; Speaking lies in hypocrisy; having their conscience seared with a hot iron; Forbidding to marry, and commanding to abstain from meats, which God hath created to be received with thanksgiving of them which believe and know the truth. For every creature of God is good, and nothing to be refused, if it be received with thanksgiving: For it is sanctified by the word of God and prayer.

1 Timothy 4:1-5

In the above verse we see that devils, or spirits, can deceive men into following demonic teachings. These doctrines forbid or bind believers in legalism, which then produces strongholds, yokes, and bondages and unscriptural mindsets. The Bible states that we are not to be conformed to this world (Satan's teachings) but to be transformed by the renewing of our minds that we may prove (accept and believe) what is God's good, acceptable and perfect will.[8] Without knowing it, many Christians have been enticed to believe doctrines of devils such as:

- accepting sickness and disease in their lives as a form of suffering for Christ;
- a poverty mentality;
- insecurities, fears, and worries.

These mindsets go against what the Bible teaches—that Jesus paid the price for our sickness and infirmities; that God has blessed us with every spiritual blessing found in heaven; and that God has not given us a spirit of fear.[9] Through the ministry of deliverance, these mindsets can be broken and believers' minds can be renewed according to the Word of God.

In deliverance ministry, binding and loosing can bring freedom to the lives of Christians who have struggled in areas of sin and bondage. Although it is available to all believers, only "those who believe" can minister effectively. However, these principles can also be used when praying for those who are not saved. For example, we might pray for an unsaved person to be delivered from drugs and alcohol: God may answer our prayer, but the person may never come to know the saving knowledge of Christ. This is something we must all consider when praying for deliverance.

Testimony

"I have noticed my lack of reacting to situations normally
where I would have felt rejected or belittled. The
situations may still occur, but I don't react the same."

Chapter 11 Binding and Loosing

1 – Mark 7:7-9
2 – John 8:43-45
3 – Matthew 23:15
4 – Matthew 16:19
5 – Acts 15:9
6 – Luke 8:27-36; 13:11-17
7 – Luke 10:18
8 – Romans 12:2
9 – Matthew 8:17; Ephesians 1:3; 2 Timothy 1:7

CHAPTER 12

Curses, Vows, and Broken Promises

Have you ever wondered why some families struggle in particular areas? Do you wonder why certain patterns exist within families? For instance, why do certain families struggle with alcohol or drug abuse? Why do patterns of sexual abuse repeat themselves from generation to generation? Why does cancer show up in one family but not another? Or why do "bad things happen to good people" for no apparent reason? Have you ever assumed heredity and genetics were responsible? In ministering inner healing and deliverance, we realize one of the reasons for the above scenarios is present day and generational curses.

The word "curse" often invokes images of shamans and witch doctors stabbing voodoo dolls with pins, and witches chanting incantations or casting evil spells. It is a word that makes our souls shudder—and rightly so. Curses are used by the devil—and by people who are being used by him—to subject us to harm, sickness, disease, and even death; as well as to shackle us in bondages, yokes, and strongholds. But did you ever think that Christians can also utter curses?

We can "word curse" each other by repeatedly speaking negative and condemning words. We might say to a child, "You're so stupid; you'll never amount to anything." Or a child may say, "I wish mom and dad would get a divorce; I hate them both!" Or a church member might declare, "My pastor is a lousy preacher; I am going to ask God to remove him from the pulpit."

From whence come wars and fightings among you? come they not hence, even of your lusts that war in your members? Ye lust, and have not: ye kill, and desire to have, and cannot obtain: ye fight and war, yet ye have not, because ye ask not. Ye ask, and receive not, because ye ask amiss, that ye may consume it upon your lusts. Ye adulterers and adulteresses, know ye not that the friendship of the world is enmity with God? whosoever therefore will be a friend of the world is the enemy of God.

James 4:1-4

Speak not evil one of another, brethren. He that speaketh evil of his brother, and judgeth his brother, speaketh evil of the law, and judgeth the law: but if thou judge the law, thou art not a doer of the law, but a judge. There is one lawgiver, who is able to save and to destroy: who art thou that judgest another?

James 4:11-12

God's Curse

In the Bible, the first curses were actually spoken by God. However, unlike our selfish motives that drive our word curses, God's curse came as a result of Adam and Eve's original sin and the deceptive work of Satan. God's curses are therefore in response to man's disobedience and doublemindedness.[1]

In Genesis 3, God pronounced three curses:
1. Satan, the serpent, was cursed above all livestock and wild animals.[2]
2. A woman's childbearing pains would be greatly increased.[3]
3. The ground would produce thorns and thistles, and man would labor under great toil to produce food.

However, God *never* cursed mankind. If you don't believe curses exist today, ask yourself two simple questions: Do women still deliver children in excruciating pain? Do men earn a living by the sweat of their brow?

The Bible further warns of potential curses:

"I call heaven and earth to record this day against you, that I have set before you life and death, blessing and cursing: therefore choose life, that both thou and thy seed may live" (Deuteronomy 30:19).

Furthermore, Deuteronomy 28 lists blessings as a result of obedience and curses occurring because of disobedience. This tells us we can choose to bless and be blessed or to curse and be cursed. Sometimes we don't realize the effects that our actions, attitudes, and words have on others and ourselves. But God wants the words of our mouths and the meditation of our hearts to be acceptable in his sight, for he is our strength and our redeemer.[4]

The Power of Words

When we repeatedly speak in negative ways or criticize others or ourselves, we are potentially releasing curses through which demons can operate against our lives as well as those of future generations. In essence, we are unwittingly being used by the devil to fulfill his purposes. Because Satan's kingdom operates on legalism, our words give him a legal right to bring harm to an individual or to ourselves.

The power of words cannot be underestimated. For instance, in the book of Numbers, King Balak, the Moabite leader, was afraid of the Israelites. He offered honor, riches, and promotion to the prophet Balaam, son of Boer, and said, "Come now therefore, I pray thee, curse me this people; for they are too mighty for me: peradventure I shall prevail, that we may smite them, and that I may drive them out of the land: for I wot that he whom thou blessest is blessed, and he whom thou cursest is cursed" (Numbers 22:6).

Noah cursed his son Canaan.[5] We can curse our parents.[6] Objects can be cursed.[7] We can curse God in our hearts.[8] We can be children of a curse.[9] These are a few examples through which our words invoke curses.

Words are a creative force; they can transmit spiritual power, blessing, and cursing. We know that God spoke the universe and the world

143

into being through his words. We, too, are spiritual beings, and our words hold the power of blessing and cursing. Scripture tells us that angels are ministering spirits sent to help believers carry out God's Word.[10] It is logical that demons hearken to our word curses, whether spoken against people or objects. For example, an abusive parent wounds his or her child through words and actions that open the child's soul to various forms of curses—from physical and emotional illness to repetitive and generational behavior patterns.

The Bible states that curses will be a reality until God returns to this earth.

"And there shall be no more curse: but the throne of God and of the Lamb shall be in it; and his servants shall serve him" (Revelation 22:3).

Because curses are one of Satan's many weapons against mankind, we must be on guard against these "bombshells from hell" we too often throw at one another. They give demonic forces legal footholds in our lives and the lives of others.

"Death and life are in the power of the tongue: and they that love it shall eat the fruit thereof" (Proverbs 18:21).

Types of Curses

In our study of the Bible, we have found fifty-nine unique types of curses and five major types that operate in this world, such as these:

1. God-given curses: God's curses are absolute, meaning they last until he decides to reverse them. We have already seen that the earth and Satan have been cursed by God. In the New Testament, Jesus cursed a fig tree that had leaves indicating it was fruitful but had no real fruit.[11]

2. Satanic curses: These are an abomination to God. They are spoken by white and black witches, warlocks and Satanists; they include hexes, vexes, spells, incantations, and jinxes.[12]

3. Disobedience curses: These always lead to sin and bring God's wrath upon the disobedient.[13]

4. Generational curses: These are passed through the bloodline and ancestral background. They include things such as diseases, iniquities, addictions, divorce, and alcoholism.[14]

144

5. Word curses: These are negative words often repeatedly spoken about an individual (i.e. gossiping) or over a person's life (i.e. directly to them).[15]

Relational Curses

Word curses can come from those who have relational authority over us. We know God has ordained that society operates on the principle of authority. In relationships between people, one's position gives him or her authority over another: a husband has authority over his wife; parents have authority over their children; and employers have authority over employees.

The relational authority between Laban, Jacob, and Rachel exemplifies the cause and effect of a curse. Laban was Rachel's father and Jacob's father-in-law. In Genesis 31, Jacob and Rachel leave Laban's home only to have him pursue them: Someone had stolen his foreign gods. When Laban caught up with and confronted Jacob, Jacob replied:

'With whomsoever thou findest thy gods, let him not live: before our brethren discern thou what is thine with me, and take it to thee. For Jacob knew not that Rachel had stolen them" (Genesis 31:32).

Jacob pronounced a judgment without knowing he was actually cursing Rachel. Later, when Rachel gave birth to Ben-Oni, she died in childbirth.

We can also look at relationships between the authorities in a child's life and the causes and effects of curses:

A mother may have three daughters. She is very proud and accepting of the first one, and she loves the fun-loving side of the third daughter. However, the mother sees too much of herself in the middle child because of her own unresolved issues. She openly rejects this daughter through statements like, "Can't you ever do anything right?" "Do you have to be so clumsy?" and "Why can't you be more like your sisters?" When the daughter reaches adulthood, she may shun relationships because her mother's words hold her in bondage. At work, she may turn down promotions because she doesn't think she is smart enough.

A teacher might say, "You're just one of those kids who will always have a hard time with math." Even though the child may be struggling in only one specific area, he or she begins to believe math will always be a tough subject.

We have all spoken curses in one form or another in our lives. And we are all subject to generational curses. A check into your family's history can reveal possible curses, such as specific illnesses and diseases, divorce, poverty, or children born out of wedlock. Outside of God-given curses, curses are not absolutes, but they can create tendencies in our lives that direct us toward certain ways of thinking or acting. They can also allow forces to operate against us that we have little control over. However, we can rise above these as we come to understand and break any curses in our lives.

Broken Promises

The best way to understand the seriousness of broken promises is through examples: There are times when we feel led to support a particular ministry, missionary organization, or individual in full-time ministry. We may sense God is speaking to us during a church service, a television or radio program, or at a special meeting. We may decide to pledge a one-time sum of money or commit to regular financial support. We may promise to pray regularly or volunteer our time to help out. But as the days go by, we "forget" our commitment. When the Holy Spirit reminds us of our commitment, we disregard his voice. In the following months, we may find out there is something wrong with the ministry or individual. There may be an ongoing investigation into misappropriation of funds. The minister may be accused of or found to be in sin. We say to ourselves, "I knew it. I knew there was a reason I was holding back on my commitment. I can't support that minister or ministry. God is exposing their sin. I would be approving of their actions or lifestyle if I send in my finances."

On the surface, our reasoning sounds logical. However, our original pledge was made not to a person or ministry but in response to the Holy Spirit asking us to commit our finances, prayer time, or physical help to God.

Aside from unforeseen emergencies, pledging and then breaking commitments of support—whether financial, prayer, or physical—is sin.

Due to laziness or critical and judgmental attitudes, we have released ourselves from a promise to God. However, we never asked God to release us. Sin is the doorway that the enemy uses to gain legal access into our lives.

"When thou shalt vow a vow unto the LORD thy God, thou shalt not slack to pay it: for the LORD thy God will surely require it of thee; and it would be sin in thee" (Deuteronomy 23:21).

Unwittingly, our broken promises may have allowed curses into our lives. They may affect our finances or cause mental distractions in our prayer times. The Bible is clear that making a vow is serious business to God. We may forget about it, but he does not. It is better not to utter a vow than to speak one and potentially curse our lives.

"When thou vowest a vow unto God, defer not to pay it; for he hath no pleasure in fools: pay that which thou hast vowed. Better is it that thou shouldest not vow, than that thou shouldest vow and not pay" (Ecclesiastes 5:4-5).

Religious Vows

Some people identify themselves not as Christians but by a particular denomination. They say, "I am committed to my church. My family has ties that go back for generations, and we're all the same religion. I was born this way and I will die this way."

As adults, we may dedicate our lives to the Church. We may take vows of poverty, chastity, or lifelong obedience and adherence to a particular set of doctrines.

Some parents dedicate their children to a particular religion or denomination. They commit their children through firsts, such as a baby confirmation or first communion, in the name of a denomination. These are forms of religious vows. On the surface, they may seem honorable and noble. God wants us to be committed to our local churches.[16] Having the self-discipline to remain faithful to what we believe is commendable. However, religious vows can bind us to a particular religion, denomination, or lifestyle. They can place bondages and commitments upon us that are not scriptural. The underlying issue is one of allegiance: God wants us to dedicate ourselves to him and him only. Religious vows are made to a church, which can lead to idolatry, allowing curses to operate in our lives. In this way the church, its rules, and its regulations take the place of God and the Bible in our lives.

Invoking a Curse

When curses are spoken, or invoked, they create openings in our lives and give demonic forces hedges (something that acts as a disguise) to operate under. Given the potential consequences of any particular curse, we doubt anyone would deliberately curse another person or their own lives. Sadly, we do exactly that. The primary way we open ourselves to potential curses is through disobedience to God's Word—in other words, through sin. There are several different ways in which curses emanate from sin:

- The Bible says that when we don't pay our tithes and offerings, we are robbing God and bringing a curse upon our lives.[17]
- We can curse ourselves through the words we speak. Rebekah wanted her son Jacob, not Esau, to receive the blessing from their father, Isaac. She sent Jacob to get a goat so that she could prepare it for Isaac.[18]
- "My father peradventure will feel me, and I shall seem to him as a deceiver; and I shall bring a curse upon me, and not a blessing. And his mother said unto him, Upon me be thy curse, my son: only obey my voice, and go fetch me them" (Genesis 27:12-13). Rebekah never saw her son Jacob alive again; she was dead by the time he returned from his self-imposed exile.
- Soulish prayers such as, "God, I ask you to punish my boss for being so mean to me" can bring curses. Too often we talk and even pray against one another. Knowingly or unwittingly, we pray from soulish emotions or demonic influence, and our words release a curse. Often, there is unforgiveness, resentment, and bitterness at the root of our prayers.
- Curses can emanate from unscriptural covenants with religions and associations that deny the divinity of Christ, that promote man's works as the way to heaven, and/or that elevate man as the ultimate authority. People in these religions and organizations

148

are committed to false gods. They are often anti-Christian and make covenants with their gods to "bring Christianity down."

- Bitter root judgments and inner vows allow demons to operate in a person's life.
- Dishonoring one's parents can cause your life to be cut short and is listed as an act of a reprobate mind and a sign of coming perilous times.[19]
- Individuals can be supernaturally empowered by Satan. These people have opened themselves up to do his bidding and allow demonic forces to operate directly through their lives. They might be witch doctors, wizards, witches, sorcerers, mediums, clairvoyants, fortunetellers, or false prophets.

Recognizing a Curse

If we cannot overcome problem areas in our lives and there is no apparent reason why, it is possible a curse is in operation. This has nothing to do with salvation and eternal life but rather with victory after salvation in this life.

A curse functions under the guise of something foreboding that we dread facing. It oppresses us, holds us back, keeps us down, or forces us to go in a direction we don't want to go in. It submerges us in a negative atmosphere that we cannot break free from. Words such as frustration, helplessness, and hopelessness may come to mind. We may even have all the tools needed to gain victory, yet something always seems to go wrong. In examining our lives, we see particular patterns of behavior or circumstances but no obvious reason for them.

We may say things like, "I remember my grandmother telling me the same thing happened to my grandfather." Our mothers may say, "The men in our family have never found steady employment." There is a sense of being victimized by something outside of our control in finances, relationships, business, or health. It is very possible the "sense" we feel is a curse in operation. Examples of present and generational curses are :

- mental and/or emotional breakdowns;
- repeated and/or chronic sickness, especially those that are hereditary;

149

- repeated miscarriage, children born out of wedlock, sometimes barrenness, adultery, and fornication;
- divorce and marital breakdowns;
- continual financial problems, especially where income appears to be sufficient;
- being accident prone;
- a history of family suicides, early deaths, or unnatural deaths.

Jesus, Our Curse Breaker

"Christ hath redeemed us from the curse of the law, being made a curse for us: for it is written, Cursed is every one that hangeth on a tree" (Galatians 3:13).

In Christ, God has made provision for every area in our lives—including setting us free from present and generational curses. How then can curses continue to plague Christians even though Jesus' finished work on the cross set us free from all curses?

Things to Consider

Jesus has redeemed us from curses that plague us, yet this does not eliminate his kingdom laws. Curses are still governed by the law of sowing and reaping. For example, God's forgiveness did not set Moses free from the sin of his anger, nor did it release King David's family from the curses of murder and adultery.

"The Lord is longsuffering, and of great mercy, forgiving iniquity and transgression, and by no means clearing the guilty, visiting the iniquity of the fathers upon the children unto the third and fourth generation" (Numbers 14:18).

Consider a father who warns his son, "If you do that, I will spank you." If the son disobeys and then asks his father for forgiveness, the father may say, "You are forgiven, but I must keep my word." If the father breaks his promise to punish, his credibility diminishes and the son's respect for him is damaged. The father must punish in spite of the fact that the son repented and was truly forgiven. No amount of good behavior, forgiveness, godly sorrow, or good intentions can bring release.

Christ did not come to free us from the law, for God has declared it good and holy.[20] But Jesus did come to redeem us from the curse of the Law that we might enjoy all the blessings of Abraham.

Paul tells us that those who "walk in the Spirit" are not subject to the Law.[21] If we perfectly obey God and live in absolute love, no harm will befall us, nor will we come under the judgment and penalties of curses. However, we have "all sinned and come short of the glory of God," both our forefathers and us.[22] More often, we walk according to our soul realm and our flesh. While we may have received forgiveness, we still remain under the consequences of sin. Forgiveness does not necessarily mean deliverance from the penalty of breaking the law; it is a separate benefit that must be claimed by faith.

Applying Christ's Benefits

At this point you might be asking, "How do I benefit from Christ's redemption from the curse?" As with all of Jesus' works, breaking curses off our lives must be done by faith; we must *apply* his finished work to our lives through faith. It is up to us to renounce any and all curses, ask for forgiveness, apply the blood, and war against the residual effects (strongholds that are mindsets) of the curses in our lives. If we do not, then we are subject to the cycles of judgment that come as consequences.

Peter wrote, "by his stripes we were healed."[23] Jesus healed us from every sickness, disease, bruise, and infirmity the enemy has brought against mankind. You may ask, "If sickness is a curse, but we are healed by the stripes of Jesus, then why are so many Christians sick?" One possible reason is because we have not learned to receive by faith the curse-breaking deliverance that Jesus freely paid the price for on our behalf.

Let's look at how this plays out in a Christian's life: We frequently forget to consult God when we are sick or injured. Or we cry out, "God, why did this happen to me? You allowed it; now heal me!" Our attitudes are wrong. Then we run to our family doctors, the local hospital, or our medicine chests. Yet God said that by the stripes of Jesus Christ we *were* healed. It is his will that we have good health. Jesus taught the twelve, then the seventy, to heal those who were sick and cast out demons. He also declared that signs shall follow those *who believe*, including healing the sick.[24] In spite of all this, we run to the doctor first instead of claiming and standing on the truth of God's Word. The doctor's report may be true. If he says we have sicknesses or illnesses, then those are what are attacking our bodies. But we allow the diagnoses to negate what God has declared. We say, "Oh well, I'm sick." However, faith says, "I may be sick, but by the stripes of Jesus I am healed."

What happens next? The negative words spoken can now become curses the enemy may use against us. A pronouncement of sickness or a dire diagnosis of disease is received as truth, which then gives the demon (a spirit of infirmity) behind the sickness the authority to bring the full effects of the curse to bear on one's life.[25] (We are not denying the reality of sickness and disease, but we want to illustrate how a word curse works.) Words are spoken that give authority to demons; that authority manifests in the form of fear, doubt, or worry.

We want to be clear: God has given us gifted men and women who work in the medical field. He has also given medical professionals the wisdom and ability to invent and develop medicines, cures for diseases, and other advancements that bring healing to society. God heals four ways: instantly, through the process of time, through doctors who provide medication and treatment, or through death—the ultimate healing. However, when we don't turn to God first, we too easily make decisions based on our emotions or what we see and hear, rather than on what God has declared to be true. This gives the enemy an enormous advantage over us.

Remember, Satan was stripped of *all* of his authority when he rebelled against God. He was completely defeated by Jesus at Calvary. So why does he continue to work effectively in our lives? Because we give him the legal right to do so through our words and our unbelief. Words are a creative force that transmits spiritual power. Even when words come from people whom we trust, they give demons the right to infiltrate our lives. When we believe a doctor's report over God's Word, it becomes "truth" to us. As we repeat the news of our malady, it gains greater authority with each repetition. What we need to say is,

"The doctor said I've got cancer, but God says by the stripes of Jesus I am healed!"

The Shunammite woman in 2 Kings 4 is a good example for us to follow: Her son died and she immediately went to see the prophet Elisha. Upon meeting him, she declared, "it is well," instead of reinforcing Satan's work in her life. She knew that God wasn't limited by her son's death and that Elisha had the faith and authority to intercede. She refused to curse herself with words that would solidify Satan's work. Instead, she agreed with Elisha's authority as he spoke the revelation God gave him. Spiritual power was released, and the boy arose to new life.

Jesus acknowledged the power of the spoken word:

"But I say unto you, That every idle word that men shall speak, they shall give account thereof in the day of judgment. For by thy words thou shalt be justified, and by thy words thou shalt be condemned" (Matthew 12:36-37).

Therefore, we must be cautious about the words we speak over others and ourselves. We can either release God's power through his Word or give Satan the legal right to bring curses.

Final Thoughts

We do not bear the guilt of our ancestors' sins, but we can potentially suffer the consequences. Curses create tendencies, drawings, and pullings in the spirit world. They are not always absolutes, except those spoken by God. God can also turn any curse into a blessing.

"Nevertheless the Lord thy God would not hearken unto Balaam; but the Lord thy God turned the curse into a blessing unto thee, because the Lord thy God loved thee" (Deuteronomy 23:5).

As for his father, because he cruelly oppressed, spoiled his brother by violence, and did that which is not good among his people, lo, even he shall die in his iniquity. Yet say ye, why? doth not the son bear the iniquity of the father? When the son hath done that which is lawful and right, and hath kept all my statutes, and hath done them, he shall surely live. The soul that sinneth, it shall die. The son shall not bear the iniquity of the father."

Ezekiel 18:18-20

Walking upright and being obedient affects everything in our lives. Biblical confessions can bring release and freedom. Jeremiah the prophet declared, "We acknowledge, O Lord, our wickedness, and the iniquity of our fathers: for we have sinned against thee" (Jeremiah 14:20).

We need to turn from sin, break the curses, confess the sins of our forefathers and ancestors, and cancel the negative effects through positive confession and profession of God's Word over our lives, circumstances, and situations.

On the cross Jesus was made a curse so that we might receive the blessing. That is already provided, but we must make it real in our personal experiences. He was punished that we might be forgiven. He was wounded that we might be healed. These are all finished works. However, in order to receive forgiveness, we must do what God requires. In order to be healed, we must proclaim God's Word. In order to be free from curses, we must appropriate God's provision in our personal lives.

Testimony

Sorrow Turned to Joy

Praise the name of the Lord Jesus Christ! (Thank you Lord God for leading me to Evangel Christian Church.)

Never have I witnessed such loyalty and dedication to God's people as I've seen in you both! The love of the Spirit shines brightly in you both and in your church. Thank you, Jesus! I give all praise, glory, and honor to the Lord, who has set me free!!! Before the seminar, I suffered from a lot of weird things. (At the time, of course, I didn't realize I was under oppression from demons; I just thought it was part of my personality). I was a lair and couldn't stop lying, no matter how hard I tried. I was a nicotine-puffing drunk who abused prescription pills. I was constantly tormented with fear, but especially at night. (I would dread going to bed and had to sleep with the light on.) I was involved in a controlling relationship that I could not

154

break from. I was insanely jealous. Lust had taken control of me, along with masturbation, fantasy, and escapism.

I could not pray because of so much static and interference; my prayer was simple: "God help me!" Mental fog, confusion, oppression, and depression actually had me under control. I didn't know how to fight it. Time was my enemy. Living was a battle. The devil took me for quite a ride! Today I suffer from none of these things. The Lord has restored my mind, body, senses, emotions—everything! He has made me whole again. He has given me my youth back, which the devil had stolen. He has given me joy where there was only sorrow. He has given me hope where there was only worry. He has given me peace where there was only trouble. And most importantly he has given me love where there was nothing!! The Lord has restored me and delivered me and saved me from the snares of the evil one. I just am in awe of his magnificence. Praise the blessed name of the Lord, from whose goodness is manifest in our presence! Our god is an awesome God! Halleluiah!

May his blessings pour abundantly on you!!!!!!

Chapter 12 Curses, Vows, and Broken Promises

1 – Deuteronomy 28:15-29;
   James 1:6-8, 22
2 – Genesis 3:14
3 – Genesis 3:16
4 – Psalm 19:14
5 – Genesis 9:25
6 – Leviticus 20:9
7 – Deuteronomy 7:26
8 – Job 1:5
9 – Peter 2:14-15
10 – Hebrews 11:14
11 – Mark 11:13-21
12 – Exodus 22:18;
   Deuteronomy 18:9-11
13 – Romans 5:19; Ephesians 5:6
14 – Exodus 20:5; 34:7
15 – Proverbs 18:21
16 – Hebrews 10:25
17 – Malachi 3:8-9
18 – Genesis 27
19 – Ephesians 6:1-3;
   Romans 1:28-30;
   2 Timothy 3:1-3
20 – Romans 7:12
21 – Galatians 5
22 – Romans 3:23
23 – 1 Peter 2:24
24 – Mark 16:15-18
25 – Luke 13:11

CHAPTER 13

Strongholds, Yokes, and Bondages

Spiritual warfare is often thought of as a unidirectional attack. We fight against powers, principalities, and rulers of this dark world. However, spiritual warfare is not one-dimensional. The Bible speaks about a second enemy that we war against:

> This I say then, Walk in the Spirit, and ye shall not fulfill the lust of the flesh. For the flesh lusteth against the Spirit, and the Spirit against the flesh: and these are contrary the one to the other: so that ye cannot do the things that ye would.
>
> Galatians 5:16-17

The flesh is as much our enemy as the demons that use it against us. Jesus came to free us from all of our enemies. Yet many believers are bound by strongholds, yokes, and bondages in their spirits and flesh (mind, will, emotions, and body). These dominate and control us like puppets on strings and become evident in our lifestyles. Satan has us convinced we have no way out, no path to freedom. His lies and deceptions are like a spider's web, entangling us in feelings of hopelessness and despair. But the Good News, the gospel of Jesus Christ, is exactly that—good news! Jesus paid the price for our freedom and wants to give us abundant life that includes shattering the strongholds, yokes, and bondages that hold us captive.

When it comes to strongholds, yokes, and bondages, there are some ministers who do not differentiate between those in our flesh and those due to demonic activity. They get "spooky spiritual" and call out demons in people's lives that don't exist. For instance, an alcoholic may be in *bondage* to alcohol. He may have *strongholds* in his mind (chemical and emotional) that drive him to drink. His thoughts and perceptions of alcohol may consume him and *yoke* him to drinking. Demons then have a legal right to influence him toward drinking, driving him further into his addiction. But there is not necessarily a demon of alcohol within him.

Misdirected warfare can be seen when praying for healing of a disease such as cancer: Cancer is a consequence of our environment, food, heredity, or other factors. While all sickness and disease are rooted in man's fall in the garden, and therefore demonic in origin, there is not necessarily a demon of cancer. Sometimes we cast out a demon of cancer, and sometimes we pray against a spirit of infirmity that can bring about cancer in our bodies. At other times, God will lead us to pray for divine healing.

How do we know whether a stronghold, yoke, or bondage results from sinful behavior, environmental or social conditions, or demonic activity? We must have a thorough understanding of spiritual warfare in order to rightly divide what is spirit from what is flesh. We need to operate in the gifts of the Spirit, such as discernment and word of knowledge. We must also "learn to discern" by listening to the voice of the Holy Spirit.

Strongholds, yokes, and bondages are real. And we all struggle with one or more of them in some areas of our lives.

Strongholds

The word "stronghold" can mean *a well-fortified city or fortress*. It can also mean *a central place of agreed-upon thoughts and views*. Strongholds conjure up images of something impregnable, rigid, and unmoving. For instance, a university may be called a stronghold of liberalism or conservatism because of its reputation for allowing liberal or conservative thinking.

On a psychological level, strongholds are an integral part of our *belief systems*. They are the driving force behind our thought patterns, attitudes, and actions. No matter what we say in everyday life or what we truly believe about the world around us—God, others, or ourselves—the strongholds in our minds come to surface when we are put in pressure situations. These can also be emotional safe havens that protect us from perceived harm. For instance, someone who fears rejection may take solace in imaginative mindsets of revenge upon those who have harmed them.

When ministers discuss strongholds, they invariably quote one particular Scripture:

For though we walk in the flesh, we do not war after the flesh: (For the weapons of our warfare are not carnal, but mighty through God to the pulling down of strong holds;) Casting down imaginations, and every high thing that exalteth itself against the knowledge of God, and bringing into captivity every thought to the obedience of Christ; And having in a readiness to revenge all disobedience, when your obedience is fulfilled.

2 Corinthians 10:3-6

In the NIV translation, these verses read thusly:

For though we live in the world, we do not wage war as the world does. The weapons we fight with are not the weapons of the world. On the contrary, they have divine power to demolish strongholds. We demolish arguments and every pretension that sets itself up against the knowledge of God, and we take captive every thought to make it obedient to Christ. And we will be ready to punish every act of disobedience, once your obedience is complete.

2 Corinthians 10:3-6

Many ministers doing deliverance quote these verses when directly engaging demons in combat. We must not forget there are demonic powers, principalities, and rulers that establish strongholds (territories) on the earth. They can manifest themselves through political parties, regimes, religions, and dictatorships. They can establish strongholds of belief that yoke countries and world regions to a particular way of thinking, such as communism. The resulting bondage is seen in poor economic growth and poverty in the lives of those living under such demonic control.

But Paul is not talking about this type of confrontation. Rather, he is discussing *strongholds* as *mindsets* that keep us in bondage. Even though demons are indirectly the cause of these and use these to gain control over our lives, in context, the strongholds Paul talks about are:

- erroneous beliefs, persuasions, and teachings that lead to "acts of disobedience" (verse 5);
- religious lies and deceptions the enemy uses to enslave us to his ways of thinking, his attitudes, and actions;
- false arguments and pretensions that come against a true understanding (the knowledge) of God.

In psychological terms, strongholds could be considered "practiced ways of habitual thinking that bind us to bad habits, addictions, and lifestyles." They can fill us with hopelessness, leading us to believe something in our lives is unchangeable. Their function is to control our thinking while minimizing anything that contradicts it.

On a demonic level, a stronghold can be defined as *an influence or grip; a persistent oppression, obsession, hindrance, or harassment.*

Examples of religious strongholds include these:

- False doctrines such as denying the divinity of Christ or advocating that man is sinless or salvation is earned.
- False teachings such as those that say God punishes us with sickness, God wants us poor, or piousness equates to material prosperity.

Examples of strongholds in the mind are stubbornness, pride, inferiority/superiority complex, confusion, prejudice, and lying. Demonic strongholds include rebellion, lust, witchcraft, idolatry, and the occult.

In Paul's day, strongholds in the mind probably included keeping certain man-made traditions or following particular rules, laws, and regulations. These were attempts to please God through "works" instead of accepting Jesus' finished work by grace. Evidently, there were some in the Corinthian church who were promoting such things as legalism over grace and permissiveness over self-discipline.

Testimony

"God gave me peace all day throughout the seminar.
The paperwork was a catharsis in itself.
I urge others to be honest in all the phases
of the paperwork."

Punishing Disobedience

What did Paul mean when he said he was "ready to punish every act of disobedience?" Let's look closer at 2 Corinthians 10:4-5: "Casting down imaginations and every high thing" (verse 4, KJV) is more accurately translated "Demolishing arguments and false pretenses" (NIV).

Paul was saying he would vigorously point out *opinions* that others were stating as *facts* about Christ. "Bringing into captivity every thought" (KJV) equates to proving the truth about Christ by rightfully dividing Scripture.

He went on to say he was ready "to revenge" (verse 5, "punish," NIV) all disobedience, when your obedience is fulfilled." In translating the Greek meanings of these words, Paul was *not* referring to physically punishing anyone. Nor was he referring to warring against demons. Instead, he was ready to defend the truth of the gospel by refuting those who taught false doctrines and teachings (all disobedience). He would do this only *after* the Corinthian church realized they had been deceived and did not have truthful or "obedient" mindsets or "strongholds" about Christ and their freedom in him.

Yokes

A yoke is something that links, enjoins, or locks two things in place, so that one cannot move without the other. Most often we see yokes used on teams of oxen or horses. In this case, the yoke is a type of harness, made of wood (oxen) or leather (horses), that forces the animals to move in tandem. One result of "yoking" animals together is that their combined strength is multiplied. For instance, a team of two workhorses yoked together can pull up to four times the weight that one horse could pull.

A yoke can also mean *a bond that is oppressive or burdensome*. Paul said this to the Corinthians:

> Be ye not unequally yoked together with unbelievers: for what fellowship hath righteousness with unrighteousness? and what communion hath light with darkness? And what concord hath Christ with Belial? or what part hath he that believeth with an infidel? And what agreement hath the temple of God with idols? for ye are the temple of the living God; as God hath said, I will dwell in them, and walk in them; and I will be their God, and they shall be my people.
>
> 2 Corinthians 6:14-16

Here we see Paul links the words yoked, common, fellowship, harmony, and agreement together. Thus, a yoke can mean *an agreement in mindsets that are evidenced in lifestyle*. Paul is telling the Corinthian church—and us—not to be joined (yoked) together in body, mind, or spirit with unbelievers. He states we have nothing in common: There is no compatibility or equality. Our lifestyles differ (fellowship); our thought lives are different (harmony); and we act differently (agreement). He warns us that joining ourselves together in any of these areas may result in grief, hardship, sorrow, and pain. This does not mean we disassociate ourselves from the world. God has called us to live in this world but not to be of this world. Jesus ate and fellowshipped with publicans and sinners yet did not acquiesce to their lifestyles for ministry and evangelism purposes.

There is also a third meaning of the word yoke: In King James English, it meant "to rob" in the sense that "two thieves yoked the man of his wallet." Whenever we are compelled to follow a particular sin or sinful lifestyle, we are *yoked or robbed* of the freedom God desires for us.

Testimony

"I encourage others to be obedient in their preparation
for the workshop.
I would not have received so much from God had I not
prepared myself properly."

Bondages

"They answered him, We be Abraham's seed, and were never in bondage to any man: how sayest thou, Ye shall be made free?" (John 8:33).

The Israelite nation was well acquainted with the word bondage. It means to be *a slave to, to serve and be subject to someone or something other than one's self.* For instance, the ancient Israelites were in bondage to the nation of Egypt, serving as their slaves and performing the most menial tasks.

Bondage can also mean *the state of being under the control of a force or influence or abstract power.* For example, "He was in bondage to fear" or "His life was bound up in sex."

The Israelites had spent their first four hundred years, before becoming a fledgling nation, as a people group in bondage to Egypt. From both written and oral traditions, they understood the slavery, torment, and subjugation that bondage brings.

Bondage is the end result of negative strongholds in our mind. We are enslaved to particular lifestyles through addictions, cravings, and inordinate desires. We cannot escape a particular bondage because we believe the mindset we established is true. For instance, we might believe sex equates to happiness, or shopping means fulfillment, or adultery will make us feel good.

Strongholds, yokes, and bondages form vicious and self-perpetuating cycles. Eventually, we are bound so tightly that it is almost impossible to break free of their hold. We are unable to accept the truths found in God's Word, or we cannot consistently follow them.

Signs to Look for

How do we know when we are faced with a stronghold, yoke, or bondage? They reveal themselves through our words and lifestyles:

- We are constantly critical of everyone and everything.
- We minimize or negate true or positive things said about us by others.
- We hide our bad habits.
- Certain thoughts fill us with shame, guilt, or condemnation.
- A particular behavior worsens over time.
- We are driven by our impulses and desires.

We are unwilling to give up particular mindsets because we find security and protection with them. They are familiar to us and we believe there is "truth" in them.

Strongholds, yokes, and bondages can vary from minor to moderate to severe. Extreme forms include mindsets that greatly hinder us spiritually, socially, or physically, such as an addiction. Moderate strongholds may limit our fulfillment in life, yet we can still function effectively. For instance, if we believe that poverty equates to pious humility, we may give all of our money away. Minor thoughts such as the need to protect ourselves by lying can be eradicated through conviction from God, leading to our confession and repentance.

Testimony

"The very act of preparation for the workshop
was truly a blessing for me."

King Saul

King Saul's life succinctly illustrates how strongholds, yokes, and bondages can develop, interact with each other, and open the doors for demons to influence our lives. After hearing continual complaints from the Israelites, God instructed Samuel to anoint Saul to be the nation's first king.[1] However, when Samuel summoned the people to Mizpah to introduce their new king, Saul was nowhere to be found; he had hidden himself amongst the baggage.[2] Why did he do this? A likely reason was he felt very insecure due to low self-esteem. Had he been a man full of self-confidence, he would have welcomed the people's accolades and basked in his kingship. Instead, insecurity and low self-esteem were established *strongholds* in his belief system. He was *yoked* to them through his thought life, thus resulting in *bondage* to fear as displayed in his decision to hide.

We can have the same type of struggles in our lives. For instance, due to fear of rejection, we may be afraid to ask someone for help, apply for a new job, or confront someone over a wrongdoing. Fears are strongholds in our belief systems (minds) that we choose to yoke ourselves to (come in agreement with). They paralyze our actions, bringing us into bondage to indecision.

A Downward Spiral

Even though Saul rescued the city of Jabesh—which should have boosted his confidence—his insecurity and low self-esteem led him to make poor spiritual decisions based on emotion rather than good decisions based on faith.[3] These decisions further reinforced his established strongholds, yokes, and bondages.

In chapter 13, Samuel instructed Saul to wait seven days for him to offer the required sacrifices to God before going to war with the Philistines. However, when Saul did not see Samuel in time and his men began to scatter, Saul took matters into his own hands. He committed the cardinal sin of assuming the position of high priest and offered up burnt offerings to God. When Samuel arrived, he was mortified:

And Samuel said, What hast thou done? And Saul said, Because I saw that the people were scattered from me, and that thou camest not within the days appointed, and that the Philistines gathered themselves together at Michmash; Therefore said I, The Philistines will come down now upon me to Gilgal, and I have not made supplication unto the LORD: I forced myself therefore, and offered a burnt offering. And Samuel said to Saul, Thou hast done foolishly: thou hast not kept the commandment of the

LORD thy God, which he commanded thee: for now would the LORD have established thy kingdom upon Israel for ever. But now thy kingdom shall not continue: the LORD hath sought him a man after his own heart, and the LORD hath commanded him to be captain over his people, because thou hast not kept that which the LORD commanded thee.

1 Samuel 13:11-14

Saul's insecurity, low self-esteem, and lack of faith led him into disobedience, resulting in sinful actions with disastrous consequences. God took away his family's right to the kingship of Israel. Saddened and downtrodden, Saul found the thought of his son, Jonathan, not following in his footsteps unbearable. When God's chosen captain of his people was revealed, Saul turned into a possessed man.

A Spirit of Torment

After David was anointed by Samuel to be Israel's next king, the Holy Spirit forsook Saul. "But the Spirit of the LORD departed from Saul, and an evil spirit from the LORD troubled him. And Saul's servants said unto him, Behold now, an evil spirit from God troubleth thee" (1 Samuel 16:14-15).

The Hebraic words *evil spirit* indicate that Saul was filled with gloom and despondency. The Holy Spirit had taken away his anointing, and grief and sorrow overwhelmed him. These new strongholds took root in his mind and further yoked him in bondage to depression that probably lasted the rest of his life. Evil spirits would have also tormented him by sending fiery darts of self-condemnation, ridicule, and despair into his mind.

Is it possible that Saul had an evil spirit? Yes. He no longer had the Holy Spirit in his life. He certainly "had a demon(s)." Ironically, it was David's musical gifting that relieved Saul's misery.

"And it came to pass, when the evil spirit from God was upon Saul, that David took an harp, and played with his hand: so Saul was refreshed, and was well, and the evil spirit departed from him" (1 Samuel 16:23).

A Root of Bitterness

Although Saul remained king until his death in battle, he no longer lived a life worthy of kingship. When David prospered in battle and won the hearts of the people, Saul became "very wroth" and was consumed with jealousy.[4] A stronghold of bitterness took root in his heart that led him into further sin.

> And it came to pass on the morrow, that the evil spirit from God came upon Saul, and he prophesied in the midst of the house: and David played with his hand, as at other times: and there was a javelin in Saul's hand. And Saul cast the javelin; for he said, I will smite David even to the wall with it. And David avoided out of his presence twice. And Saul was afraid of David, because the LORD was with him, and was departed from Saul.
>
> 1 Samuel 18:10-12

The Amplified Bible interprets the word "prophesy" as *raved madly*. Tormented by shame, guilt, and anguish, Saul mercilessly hunted David at every opportunity. Saul must have believed the only way for him to regain peace in his life and to keep the kingship within his family was to kill David. His hatred for David so consumed him that he even tried to kill Jonathan when Jonathan defended David.[5] Saul finally took his own pitiful life by falling on his sword after being severely wounded in battle at the hands of his archenemies, the Philistines.

An Overcomer

In context of deliverance, strongholds are mindsets that "yoke or join" us together with religious teachings (false doctrines and teachings), unhealthy thought patterns (pride and jealousy), or demonism (rebellion and witchcraft). These can bring grief or sorrow into our lives and rob us of the freedom Christ wants us to have.

"Nay, in all these things we are more than conquerers through him that loved us" (Romans 8:37).

As Christians, we are "in Christ" and have the ability to overcome any obstacles in our lives. The Bible states that we have the mind of Christ.[6] We are more than conquerors: We are overcomers. We can refute, negate, and break strongholds, yokes, and bondages in our minds and lives through the power of the Holy Spirit, the Word of God, and submitting ourselves to the Lordship of Jesus.

We do not overcome strongholds, yokes, and bondages simply by rebuking demonic spirits. Nor do we overcome them by "proving our point" to others through arguments and fights. On the contrary, our weapons are not carnal, but mighty through God, enabling us to pull these down. Our spiritual weapons include these:

- Prayer[7]
- Fasting[8]
- Quoting scriptures[9]
- Obedience to God's Word[10]
- Living by faith[11]
- Walking in love[12]

No matter what the stronghold is, we must take our thoughts captive, making them obedient to Christ in every situation. Doing so destroys the yoke (agreement) we have with the mindset we want to break. This will eventually lead to freedom from the bondages we are enslaved to. Submitting ourselves to God allows the Holy Spirit's anointing to flow in our lives. And where the anointing is—there is freedom.

"Yet the defenced city shall be desolate, and the habitation forsaken, and left like a wilderness: there shall the calf feed, and there shall he lie down, and consume the branches thereof" (Isaiah 27:10).

Testimony

"We were all together in one room and at no
time were we separated.
First we had inner healing, then we were
ministered to in deliverance.
My husband and I felt so free!
We experienced such cleansing, and we've
never been the same."

Chapter 13 Strongholds, Yokes, and Bondages

1 – 1 Samuel 10:1
2 – 1 Samuel 10:22
3 – 1 Samuel 11
4 – 1 Samuel 18:6-9
5 – 1 Samuel 20:30-33
6 – 1 Corinthians 2:16
7 – Matthew 17:21
8 – Matthew 17:21
9 – Matthew 4:1-4
10 – Romans 6:16
11 – Hebrews 11:1
12 – 2 John 1:6

CHAPTER 14

Detestable Objects and Spiritual Housecleaning

Testimony

"There is no bigger thrill than seeing someone who comes in struggling and not knowing what to do, and then watching them leave the seminar totally free!"

In the Old Testament, God was very explicit regarding his thoughts on detestable objects and spiritual housecleaning. To understand what detestable objects are and why we need to perform periodic spiritual housecleaning, we need to know what God said to the Israelites. Our goal should be to remove anything from our homes that doesn't please God.

While the Israelites waited in the Plains of Moab to cross the Jordan River, Moses delivered his farewell sermon—the book of Deuteronomy. This book is aptly called "the second law" because it repeats many of the laws previously given to the Israelites, including the Ten Commandments. The book's message is pressing and urgent: It emphasizes the sober reality of God's blessings and curses. With great passion, Moses urged the Israelites (and us) to be completely loyal to God and not deviate from his laws.

"For the LORD thy God walketh in the midst of thy camp, to deliver thee, and to give up thine enemies before thee; therefore shall thy camp be holy: that he see no unclean thing in thee, and turn away from thee" (Deuteronomy 23:14).

In Deuteronomy 7, Moses proclaimed that God would bring the Israelites into the land before them and defeat the nations that are "mightier than you."[1] He then listed warnings and judgments that would befall God's people if they followed the pagan ways of the nations that were about to be driven out. He cautioned:

"Neither shalt thou bring an abomination into thine house, lest thou be a cursed thing like it: but thou shalt utterly destest it, and thou shalt utterly abhor it; for it is a cursed thing" (Deuteronomy 7:26).

God was making a clear statement. Idols, graven images, or anything copied or taken from pagan nations was detestable to him. The Israelites were to love what God loved and hate what he hated. He was adamant in his direction to the Israelites, and his admonitions apply to us. He wants us to remove detestable objects from our homes so we can be free to love and serve him wholly.

A Biblical Look

When the Israelites left Egypt and crossed over the Red Sea, God gave Moses the Ten Commandments. First and foremost he told them:

Thou shalt have no other gods before me. Thou shalt not make unto thee any graven image, or any likeness of any thing that is in heaven above, or that is in the earth beneath, or that is in the water under the earth: Thou shalt not bow down thyself to them, nor serve them: for I the LORD thy God am a jealous God, visiting the iniquity of the fathers upon the children unto the third and fourth generation of them that hate me; And shewing mercy unto thousands of them that love me, and keep my commandments.

Exodus 20:3-6

The Israelites owed their allegiance to God alone. However, as they so quickly proved when they made the golden calf, their hearts were easily led astray.[2] Idols or graven images were created things, and Israel was to worship their Creator, not creation. Images retained from pagan nations would only gratify and magnify their covetousness. God warned:

"Thou shalt not desire the silver or gold that is on them, nor take it unto thee, lest thou be snared therein" (Deuteronomy 7:25).

The story of Achan is a perfect example of God's seriousness toward detestable objects.[3] In an act of covetousness, Achan took some of the devoted things dedicated to the Lord after Jericho was captured. His sin affected the nation: They lost their next battle at Ai. When Joshua petitioned, the Lord said to Joshua, "Get thee up; wherefore liest thou thus upon thy face? Israel hath sinned, and they have also transgressed my covenant which I commanded them; for they have even taken of the accursed thing, and have also stolen, and dissembled also, and they have put it even among their own stuff" (Joshua 7:10-11).

By lot, Achan was found out and put to death. Like Achan, when we have things in our homes that do not please God, we bring judgment upon ourselves. These can also be legal access for demons to enter and attack our lives.

Idolatry

To commit idolatry means to *perform an act of worship toward any created thing; to believe that a particular created thing is an independent power;* or *to make something a mediator between ourselves and the Almighty.* We commit idolatry whenever we value something or someone in a way that puts it or him or her above our love for and our trust in God. We give honor to something or someone that really belongs to God. Idolatry tears down our desire to put God first in our lives.[4] In our society, we idolize people such as athletes, actors and actresses, and other public figures. We say things like, "I wish I were him or her." We try to emulate our idols and buy products endorsed by them. But God alone deserves our hearts.

Putting God first means to love and trust him above all.[5] Doing so means we can love others and ourselves freely, because loving God first

173

brings balance to our other relationships. There is a difference between *admiring* someone and *idolizing* them. There is also a difference between *aspiring to be like* someone and *wanting to be* that person. When our hearts are devoted to God and he is the object of our worship, we will have balanced views and attitudes toward other people.

Covetousness

Covetousness and idolatry go hand-in-hand. The Tenth Commandment states:

"Thou shalt not covet thy neighbour's house, thou shalt not covet thy neighbour's wife, nor his manservant, nor his maidservant, nor his ox, nor his ass, nor any thing that is thy neighbour's" (Exodus 20:17).

The word "covet" means to *wish for earnestly; to desire (what belongs to another) inordinately or culpably; to feel inordinate desire for what belongs to another*. We can desire something without coveting it. Paul exhorts us to "Follow after charity, and *desire* spiritual gifts, but rather that ye may prophesy" (1 Corinthians 14:1, italics added). When we desire something, we seek earnestly after it. But desire can easily turn into coveting. When our thoughts are *consumed* by someone or something other than by God, our desire becomes inordinate, and we covet.

Another word for covet is *greed*.

From whence come wars and fightings among you? come they not hence, even of your lusts that war in your members? Ye lust, and have not: ye kill, and desire to have, and cannot obtain: ye fight and war, yet ye have not, because ye ask not. Ye ask, and receive not, because ye ask amiss, that ye may consume it upon your lusts.

James 4:1-3

This verse illustrates the result of coveting and greediness. Covetousness poisons our hearts, turns us away from God, and causes division and dissension in our relationships.

Testimony

"I know that God did a work in me during
the entire seminar.
I am most grateful for the follow-up policy;
it keeps me on course."

Detestable Objects

The words abominable (KJV) and detestable (NIV) are interchangeable. In fact, most dictionaries will use these words as synonyms. They both mean *worthy of and/or causing intense hatred*. What objects are detestable to God? The Bible gives us some examples:

- God told the Israelites to "Bring no more vain oblations; incense is an abomination to me; the new moons and sabbaths, the calling of assemblies, I cannot away with; it is iniquity, even the solemn meeting" (Isaiah 1:13).
- Jesus said to the Pharisees, who loved money, "Ye are they which justify yourselves before men; but God knoweth your hearts: for that which is highly esteemed among men is abomination in the sight of God" (Luke 16:15).
- Paul stated, "Unto the pure all things are pure: but unto them that are defiled and unbelieving is nothing pure; but even their mind and conscience is defiled" (Titus 1:15).

Things that are detestable to God include lying lips, disobedience, evil sacrifices and idolatry, rebellion, pride, dishonesty, and *objects in our possession that do not glorify him.*[6]

Spiritual Housecleaning

As Christians, we want to please God in everything we do. We don't say, "I think I'll covet today. I'm going to buy something that is detestable to God and keep it in my house." We do not deliberately sin.

"Whosoever is born of God doth not commit sin; for his seed remaineth in him: and he cannot sin, because he is born of God" (1 John 3:9).

175

However, through ignorance or unbelief, we may allow things into our homes that do not please God. We may buy something we feel is harmless but in reality may be an accursed thing. Depending on its origin, the object may actually carry a curse or house an unclean spirit. The object may also have had hexes, vexes, spells, or incantations spoken over them. These can be sources of such things as headaches, illness, disease, sleepless nights, nightmares, and family arguments. It is important, therefore, to do periodic *spiritual housecleaning*. This means we are going to first examine our hearts to see if we've set anyone above God in our lives. (Our body is the temple or house of the Holy Spirit.[7]) Then, prayerfully, we go through each room of our homes, asking the Lord if the room contains anything that doesn't please him.

Purification Process

To help search our hearts and homes for that which displeases God, we have developed a purification process. We suggest the following steps:

1. *Seek Forgiveness and Repent.* Whether we have made someone an idol in our hearts or brought a detestable object into our homes, whenever we idolize something, we commit idolatry. We must ask God to forgive us for setting the created above the Creator. We then repent by making a decision to give up our idolatry and remove any "graven images" that God shows us from our homes.

2. *Remove all items and destroy them.* After God shows us any detestable objects, we are to "la[y] them out before the Lord."[8] We strongly advise against selling items or giving them away. Why would we want to bring a curse into someone else's life? "Many of them also which used curious arts brought their books together, and burned them before all men: and they counted the price of them, and found it fifty thousand pieces of silver. So mightily grew the word of God and prevailed" (Acts 19:19-20).

> *Singular sin brings plural guilt.*

3. *Dedicate ourselves and our homes to the Lord.* To dedicate means to set apart for service.

4. *Repent on behalf of others who have brought idolatry into our homes.* This includes friends, family, and previous homeowners or renters.

5. *Break any unknown ties.* Remember, a curse or demon has a right to stay in place until we renounce and rebuke it.

6. *Cover with the blood of Jesus.* Neither demons nor curses can stay in the presence of Jesus' blood. They must flee!

7. *Consecrate our homes to the Lord.* We sanctify our homes and make them holy places for the Holy Spirit to dwell. We must dedicate all that is in our homes to his glory and set it all apart for his use.

8. *Anoint and Pray.* We pray through each room in our homes, binding and casting out any spirits that may be dwelling there, and anoint the external and internal doorways and windows with oil. Anointing oil is a symbolic way of setting our homes apart for the Lord.

Singular sin brings plural guilt. Detestable objects are no different than acted out sins. When we allow these to stay in our homes, they affect everyone who dwells in them.

Words of Caution

When seeking God for direction about what to remove from our homes, we caution against debating what comes to mind. We have to trust that God is leading and simply get rid of what he shows us. If we wait, the enemy will try to convince us that God isn't speaking and that there is nothing wrong with what we are supposed to remove. Sometimes an object doesn't seem ungodly. However, if the Holy Spirit says it must go, then go it must.

Oftentimes, we are asked what to do when a family member is keeping an accursed object. Wisdom is needed. Remember, God will show us the possessions we need to remove. We can deal with only what belongs to us. If, for instance, you feel your spouse has something that is not pleasing to God, then you should talk to him or her about it. If your spouse doesn't agree or won't even listen, then you can anoint the object with oil and pray over it.

Previously, a member of our church anointed her husband's "detestable" pictures in his workshop and his rock-and-roll albums with oil, then prayed over them. Within a month he threw them all out. He claimed he didn't even know why he had kept them.

If we have teenagers, they may have all sorts of idolatrous paraphernalia. Talking to them about these and how the Lord views them is the best idea. However, most teenagers will say something like, "Quit being such a fanatic. It's my room, and I can do what I want." How you deal with your teenager will depend on your relationship with him or her and the authority you have in your own house. If you feel you will start World War III, then our advice is to anoint the teen's room with oil, pray over it, and leave the results to God.

When it comes to children, we have the right to remove what we feel led to. If the child is old enough to understand, we should explain why we are taking away his or her toy or object. Sometimes we must be willing to apologize and ask the child's forgiveness for allowing something into their lives that doesn't please God. Then we must replace it with something of equal or greater value.

What Defiles

Oftentimes, we do not realize we have allowed things that defile into our homes. Sometimes there are unexplained "happenings" with no obvious cause.

For instance, we were asked to come to the home of a lady who had been suffering from migraine headaches for several years. She was a deaconess and a strong believer in Christ. Her doctor could find no cause, nor did any of her prescribed medications work. As soon as I walked into her living room, my eyes were drawn to a flower vase.

"Where did that come from?" I asked the lady.

"I bought it while in the Haitian Islands one summer while on a missions trip," she replied.

"Well, I suggest you get rid of it."

We prayed, broke the curse over the home, and commanded the demon to leave, which had legal right to stay and vex (torment) the woman through her migraines. She threw out the vase that same day and her migraines ceased.

Countries such as Haiti and India, and regions such as the Far East, are known for witchcraft, incantations, curses, and spells. These can be imparted through the laying on of hands. When purchasing items, it's important to know their countries of origin, as this lady's experience shows. Other symptoms of "spiritual pollution" in your home may include sudden or ongoing illness, nightmares, insomnia, behavioral/relational problems, a lack of peace, disturbed children, unexplained foul odors, apparitions or poltergeists, atmospheric heaviness, and continual nausea or headaches.

There are some obvious things that are detestable to God. Here is a partial list:

- Ouija boards, tarot cards, and similar "games." These are overtly demonic.
- "Dungeons and Dragons" board games or similar role-playing games. These games use real demon names. They are summoned when called on and act as spirit-guides. The players draw on a demon's knowledge and strength, giving the demon a legal right to stay even after the role-playing stops.
- Some Near- and Far Eastern artifacts.
- Some North American Indian and East Indian artifacts.
- Books on Satanism, witchcraft, and crystals. When studying such things as the occult, Satanism, demons, witches, and warlocks, you should always use a copy of text, an excerpt, or a rewrite. The writers of the original copies can attach spells, curses, and hexes; and evil transferences can be intentionally spoken over the pages to be released when the writing is opened. (This does not apply to books written by Christians on these subjects.)
- Obsessions with owls and similar birds. The Bible calls certain types of these "unclean," and they are often used in black magic. This includes creating them in certain jewelry, pendants, crystals, and other such artifacts.

- Obelisk objects such as the male phallic (loin) symbol. One pastor actually had these symbols etched in the stained glass over his baptistery and didn't even know what it meant.
- Astrology, zodiac signs, and horoscopes.
- Certain CDs, videos, video games, magazines, posters, and rock-and-roll music. Many musicians and video game designers are fully aware of the tradeoff they make for their success. Some are practicing full-blown witchcraft.
- Jehovah's Witnesses, Mormonism, Masonry, Eastern Star, and other such cults.
- Certain children's books. It is important to know the history of the stories we are reading to our children. The Harry Potter series is a good example.
- Certain jewelry. A lot of jewelry is made into symbols. Our general rule is, "If we don't know what it means, we don't buy it."
- Things that represent ungodly soul ties such as old pictures of sinful relationships or activities, and gifts from past relationships that were ungodly (roses in books, pictures, and jewelry). These reinforce the established soul tie and must be removed.
- Things with unknown history such as furniture or gifts passed down from generation to generation.
- Anything else that the Holy Spirit brings to mind.

Any of these items may give demons and curses a legal right to enter and remain in our homes, and harass our families and us. It's up to us to ask the Lord what displeases him and remove whatever he shows, therefore denying the devil any place in our lives.

Testimony

"Thanks, Pastor Jerry, for the preparation and education
you gave all of us!"

Chapter 14 Detestable Objects and Spiritual Housecleaning

1 – Deuteronomy 7:1

2 – Exodus 32; Deuteronomy 9:7-17

3 – Joshua 7

4 – Exodus 20:3-5; Deuteronomy 5:7-9;
Romans 1:21-23

5 – Deuteronomy 6:5; Matthew 22:37;
Mark 12:30; Luke 10:27

6 – Proverbs 12:22, 15:8-9, 15:26, 17:15, 28:9;
Deuteronomy 22:5, 25:13-16

7 – 1 Corinthians 6:19

8 – Joshua 7:22-23

CHAPTER 15

Methods and Techniques

Testimony

I thank the Lord Jesus Christ for both of you and the ministry at Evangel Christian Church.

I am much more aware of and in tune with the Holy Spirit than ever before! I have a greater discernment of spiritual darkness, and the tricks of our enemy, Satan. That's why I thank the Lord for the inner healing and deliverance ministry. But most of all, I want to thank both of you for your commitment and obedience to the Lord, and for the love you give so freely to all of us! I also want to thank you for all of the encouraging letters you have sent me through the past two years that I have served with you in the work of the ministry. I cannot thank you or the Lord enough. Praise and honor and glory to Him forever and ever. Amen!

Many times we are asked, "Who is qualified to minister deliverance? Church leadership? Seasoned Christians? Only those who are trained?" We are also asked, "What methodology is correct?" In other words, is there a right and wrong way to cast out a demon?

Over the years, we've found that every deliverance ministry has its own slant or standard on who can minister and what specific methods should be used. Some limit deliverance ministry to those who have completed in-depth, in-house teachings and seminars. Others feel this ministry is limited to credintialed ministers or those who serve in ministry full time. Still others state that only those who are "called, anointed, and appointed" by God can perform deliverance.

In our years of ministry, we have worked with deliverance ministers from many denominations who use varying methods and techniques. We have seen many ministries that are effective and some that are not. We are not called to judge who is right or wrong. But we do have a simple test to determine a ministry's effectiveness: The Bible says, "By their fruits ye shall know them."[1]

The track record for our ministry extends over thirty years, and thousands of people have participated in our monthly seminars. Christians have attended from all over the United States and Canada, as well as from Korea, Japan, China, Africa, and other countries. Many are high-profile pastors and leaders, while countless participants are lay ministers or believers not yet involved in formal service. Month after month, there is a waiting list for those wanting to be set free from strongholds, yokes, bondages, hurts, wounds, and demonic oppression in their lives. We do very little advertising, and our seminars are filled mainly through word-of-mouth as people share the breakthroughs they have received. The power of the Holy Spirit has given us tremendous success in seeing people set free, with hundreds of written testimonies to validate God's work. Here are our views and insights regarding the ministry of deliverance, including an overview of our seminar:

Qualifications

Often the ministry of deliverance is limited to a "chosen few" at a given church. These people are personally known to the pastor or church leader and may have taken extensive classes on deliverance methodology. We agree that those who oversee this ministry must be seasoned, mature Christians who have a devoted walk with the Lord. Make no mistake—overseeing this ministry is not for the faint-hearted. The devil will do all he can to "steal, kill and destroy" those involved. Those who oversee deliverance must be ready for personal and ministry attacks on all levels. Satan hates this ministry and will do all he can to discredit and destroy anyone involved in it. Deliverance leaders must know their authority and position in Christ, and be submitted to the Holy Spirit, allowing his gifts to flow through them.

However, we do not feel those who actually administer deliverance need to have years of experience and teaching in order to be successful. After our seminar is finished, we encourage all who have attended to come back and minister to others the following month. If this happens, they are paired with someone with more experience. The new workers act as intercessors for those receiving ministry, so that they can learn from the more experienced workers. They can also develop their gifts of the Spirit while they are in training. We activate the new workers as soon as possible by encouraging them to stretch their faith and believe that God will work through them to set others free.

When Jesus initially sent out the seventy, he gave them "power and authority" over the enemy.[2] Later, they came back rejoicing over the fact that "even the devils are subject unto us through thy name."[3] These men were not the twelve "elite" disciples, and it can be said they were not even filled with the Holy Spirit. However, they had authority from Jesus.

Concerning disciples, Jesus said, "Among them that are born of women there hath not risen a greater than John the Baptist: notwithstanding he that is least in the kingdom of heaven is greater than he" (Matthew 11:11).

The truth is that *all* believers have the authority to cast out devils. If we wait until we "feel" we are ready or for someone else to judge us as mature, we will miss out on God's equipping and using us for his glory.

Testimony

I was not sure what to say about my experience in the deliverance seminar at first, but now the results are becoming increasingly clear. I must say that, for me, everything was very quiet! While I waited to go through the seminar, I read a number of the recommended books, read my Bible, prayed, and played my praise music tapes. In addition to this, I have been through seven sessions of inner healing. This was a great deal of help to my prayer life and the practice of deliverance principles here at home for me and my husband. This has resulted in a more peaceful home life for both of us. Now from several sides, I am increasingly confronted by difficulties; however, I seem to be able to deal with them with a surprising amount of calm and effectiveness. The fruit of the Spirit (especially love, longsuffering, forgiveness, and patience) amaze me. I don't mean to say I am being perfect—far from it—but I am not thrown off balance. Praise God! I am now looking forward to increasing participation in this ministry and am in support of Evangel and its programs. Thank you for your love, thank you for your faithfulness, thank you for teaching the Word, thank you for hard work and devotion to HIM! God bless you!

Accountability

It is important that all deliverance be conducted in a safe environment, for both the person receiving ministry and the person conducting it. This includes being accountable to a local church body. Accountability is of utmost importance for several reasons:

- If you are a pastor of a local church conducting deliverance, your board, your elders, or those closest to you should be your prayer covering. We believe in a corporate anointing, and thus we do not hold private sessions or conduct them outside of the church. When we have a "lone ranger" mentality, we can easily be tripped up by the devil.
- Leaders overseeing deliverance should be accountable to their senior pastors on every issue—from members who are on the ministry team to the use of building facilities. Upward communication to the senior pastor is critical in keeping him or her abreast of the details. This provides protection and closes the door on the enemy's schemes to discredit or even bring down the ministry through gossip, slander, or similar means.
- Team leaders are set in place to monitor sessions, assist less experienced workers, and to be the "eyes and ears" of the person overseeing the seminar. They are point people that others can report to, ask questions of, and count on for support during the sessions. The overseer and all leaders must have the senior

pastor's mindset on protocol and follow it without hesitation. In a ministry of this nature, structure and organization are key.

Seminar Overview

Many times, those who minister inner healing and deliverance do so in a private setting—perhaps in a church office or at someone's home. This type of environment offers a sense of security and privacy. People can also be prayed for at a church altar in response to a pastor's invitation. We often have such altar calls at our church. However, we have found the corporate setting of our seminar to be the most effective. Here is an overview of our seminar.

Saturday Morning

On Saturday morning, we conduct an in-depth Bible-based teaching, expounding on inner healing and deliverance. Experienced ministers teach line-upon-line, precept-by-precept, so those attending are assured that inner healing and deliverance are found in God's Word. After a short introduction the teachers cover such topics as these:
- God's speaking to all of us
- the ministries of inner healing and deliverance
- forgiveness, repentance, and faith
- curses and vows
- habits versus demons
- soul ties
- detestable objects
- traumatic experiences, hurts, and wounds
- how demons can enter
- deliverance as a tool of sanctification
- biblical demonic manifestations
- Jesus' encounters with demonic spirits as recorded in the Bible

Attendees are encouraged to take notes throughout the teaching, gaining insight and revelation into familiar passages of Scripture. After the teaching session, the attendees feel confident they are in God's timing and place for their lives.

Saturday Afternoon and Evening

Praise, Testimonies, and Paperwork

Praise and prayer are powerful forerunners for inner healing and deliverance. On Saturday morning, ministers and attendees gather in the sanctuary and begin their day with up to two hours of worship and brief testimonies. Next, the two groups are separated. The attendees gather in a room to complete a package of paperwork that covers their in-depth spiritual histories on everything from past and present relationships to involvement in the occult. We allow two-and-a-half hours to complete the paperwork, including scriptures to read and prayers to pray out loud. The attendees are encouraged to be completely honest as they fill out the pages. They are assured that their paperwork is kept strictly confidential. The information recorded is not shared with anyone, including their mates. We also require a signed document stating each attendee's voluntary involvement in receiving ministry and a waiver of liability. In the meantime, the ministers are reviewing ministry techniques, praying, and interceding for the upcoming sessions. Throughout this time, there is an increase in the Holy Spirit's anointing as everyone prepares themselves for the upcoming sessions.

Communion

After completing their paperwork, the attendees gather together in the sanctuary and ministers are assigned to each of them. There is a short teaching on the importance of forgiveness and communion, then communion is served. During this time, the ministers pray specific warfare prayers over the attendees.

Breaking Curses

Following communion, time is taken to break specific personal and generational curses. We call this *stand up/sit down*. We have created a list of thirty-two potential curses that are common in our society and are included in the attendees' paperwork packets. For example, a minister leading the session will ask the attendees, "Have you ever denied the birth or the resurrection of Christ? Yes or No." Those who answered yes will stand up, and another minister leads them in a short renunciation. The minister will say, "In the name of Jesus, we break every curse of denial, deception, and spiritual blindness. We command spirits of denial, deception, and spiritual blindness to go, in Jesus' name!" The attendees who stood then sit down, and the next curse is addressed.

Womb Prayer

After breaking generational and inherited curses, the attendees are seated with their eyes closed. A minister then reads through a "womb prayer" that takes about twenty minutes. This prayer is powerful because attendees can "see" in their mind's eyes what happens during each month of their growth from conception to full-term baby. During this time, God shows each attendee that he or she is wonderfully and powerfully created, is divinely known by God, and is completely accepted by Jesus.[4] We are grateful to the Lord for giving this prayer to author Rita Bennett.[5]

Inner Healing

The hour-and-a-half inner healing portion of the seminar begins in early afternoon. Attendees gather in one room, and each is paired with two or three ministers. Attendees are asked to keep their eyes closed as the ministers review recorded memories with them, asking Jesus to bring healing. During this time, the lies of the enemy are exposed, forgiveness is applied, and Jesus brings healing to the roots of the wounds.

Deliverance

Deliverance sessions run for approximately three consecutive hours immediately following inner healing. Attendees are seated with their ministers, keeping their eyes open and fixed on the person in front of them. Ministers then call out demons in an authoritative and repetitive manner according to what they sense, feel, or see by the Holy Spirit's leading.

Attendees are forewarned not to become preoccupied with the *names* being called out. A spirit can be affecting the person directly; can come in through a curse, stronghold, or bondage; or may be generational. In the latter case an attendee may not be aware of a particular spirit that has been assigned against him or her and may not struggle with a particular issue. For example, at one seminar a minister called out a "spirit of suicide" while ministering to a young man in his twenties. He had never struggled with suicidal thoughts but found out later his grandfather had hung himself, something that had been kept secret by his parents.

Filling the House

In early evening, attendees are given their final teaching to wrap up the seminar. They are taught how to maintain their inner healing and deliverance, about beneficial changes that will occur, and about things to expect in the coming weeks. They are also taught what to avoid in order to stop the enemy from infiltrating their lives in the areas they have received healing. This teaching is the most important part of the seminar. Without it the attendee's "spiritual house" is swept clean but is empty.[6] We instruct all attendees to take one hour and fifteen minutes every day (in manageable blocks of time) for the following forty days to refill themselves with the presence of the Holy Spirit through prayer, Bible reading, and worship. We call this *Filling the House*. Attendees are also told they have received spiritual surgery that can be compared to physical surgery: A healing period exists, and extra care needs to be taken to protect what has been received.

During the final teaching, attendees are reminded about the necessity of ongoing forgiveness. They will also be more sensitive to inner healing issues that the Holy Spirit brings to their minds and will have a heightened awareness of the enemy's potential attacks on their lives. They will understand that these are the enemy's attempts to negate the healing they have received. But God will also use these to help the attendees see the woundedness of others, sharpening their gifts of discernment while making them more sensitive to hearing the Holy Spirit's voice. They will find reading their Bibles a greater joy as God gives them new insights and revelations that results in deeper walks with him.

Attendees are warned against becoming "ministers of correction." They are encouraged to quickly let go of divisive issues and avoid engaging the enemy through arguing with others and pointing out their faults. Additionally, they are cautioned against telling their own pastors they must believe in these ministries or telling their pastors how to minister inner healing and deliverance.

Often, those who receive inner healing and deliverance—because of the freedom they have personally received—want to tell everyone of their need for these. They may also see "demons under every rock" or feel the need to cast demons out of everyone or everything. Neither of these is necessarily true. Wisdom is needed when the newly delivered tell others the details of their freedom. We encourage attendees to soak in the healing they have received and allow God to give them opportunities to tell others.

Testimony

I want to give testimony to the overwhelming sense of the love and tenacity of Jesus that I felt from those who ministered inner healing and deliverance to me. I have two primary after-effects of that day! Fourteen days after the workshop, I saw and was delivered from an emotional soul tie with my sister. This unknowingly held us both in bondage and maintained a foundation of insecurity within me. Secondly, I can no longer give in to periods of doubt, self-pity, questioning, unbelief, or double-mindedness regarding my life but am wholeheartedly and daily pressing in to the fulfillment of His written and rhema Words.

Seminar Order

The order of our seminar is purposely planned. Each section builds upon the previous so attendees receive maximum benefit.

- *Praise and worship* silences the enemy's voice in the attend-ees' minds. As they pour out their hearts before God, attendees are reminded that God is in control of their lives and circumstances. Praise and worship also washes off the "dirt" that life often brings, including any recent demonic attacks. Attendees feel refreshed and open to what God has planned for them. They can focus on the ministry they will receive without being distracted by events of past weeks.
- The seminar *paperwork* "primes the pump." It allows attendees to see where, when, and how the enemy has gained legal footholds into their lives through sin, experiences, and circumstances.
- *Oral renunciations and confessions* build up the attendees' spirits. These are spoken while filling out their paperwork and during stand up/sit down. These help the attendees feel confident in God's ability to work on their behalf and prepares them for their inner healing and deliverance sessions.
- *Breaking of curses* comes before inner healing and deliverance to appropriate the blood of Jesus toward any generational iniquities.
- Taking *communion* allows attendees to examine their hearts for unforgiveness and confess it to God.
- *Inner healing* closes the legal access the enemy had in the attendees' lives while allowing God to heal their broken hearts and wounded spirits.
- *Deliverance* then becomes more effective because of the areas previously dealt with.

Chapter 15 Methods and Techniques

1 – Matthew 7:16, 20
2 – Luke 10:19
3 – Luke 10:17
4 – Psalm 139:13; Jeremiah 1:5
5 – Rita Bennett, *You Can Be Emotionally Free*, Bridge-Logos, 1982, 2001, 2005
6 – Matthew 12:43-45

CHAPTER 16

The Aftermath

Testimony

Freedom and Physical Healing

Praise God for friends in Christ. Thank God for giving you a deliverance ministry. My husband and I went through the deliverance and inner healing seminar. We already were having Bible study but, thanks be to God, after deliverance we have extended with our tongue praise, silence, and Bible study following your guidelines. Now I am free to praise God at church and home; before, I was very cold. I also went to our family doctor last Thursday who was supposed to remove some skin tumors, but he said to wait until the pap test came back. Praise God—I am healed from them! Our daughter is already preparing for the next workshop. I also want to thank God for workers and all who were a part of our deliverance. May God continue to bless you richly.

Ministering inner healing and deliverance to others is a privilege that God gives to the Body of Christ. Believers gain victory over areas in their lives they have struggled with, in some cases for years. Just as we receive spiritual freedom through a combination of faith and action, we must maintain it the same way.

After receiving inner healing and deliverance, the forty days following are of utmost importance. Just as Satan left Jesus *for a season* after tempting him in the wilderness, demons will look for opportune times to return as well.[1] It is incumbent upon each of us to stand fast in our faith, submit to God, and resist the temptation to fall back into old habits and patterns.

A Serious Matter

Deliverance from demonic contamination is a process. Jesus said, "Ye shall know the truth, and the truth shall *make* you free," not *set* you free (John 8:32, italics added). (To be "made free" is an ongoing process; to be "set free" indicates a one-time experience.) God wants to restore our souls.[2] This means he returns our souls to their original condition over time.

It is important to understand that in order to maintain spiritual freedom, our undivided attention must be firmly fixed upon the person and Lordship of Jesus Christ. Should we choose to go back to sinful ways, the unclean spirits will return and try to force us into bondage once again.

"When the unclean spirit is gone out of a man, he walketh through dry places, seeking rest, and findeth none. Then he saith, I will return into my house from whence I came out; and when he is come, he findeth it empty, swept, and garnished. Then goeth he, and taketh with himself seven other spirits more wicked than himself, and they enter in and dwell there: and the last state of that man is worse than the first" (Matthew 12:43-45).

The first step in maintaining our freedom is to guard our thought lives. Evil or unclean thoughts are not sin, but meditating on them leads to sin.[3] The battleground is in the mind, and habits and patterns must be broken. Anything that constitutes sin in any form must be stopped at once. After receiving inner healing and deliverance, we become extremely sensitive to the spirit world (the kingdom of darkness) and aware of temptation. We cannot get away with any kind of sin—things we know to be wrong yet willfully keep doing—without consequences.

The Aftermath

Monitoring Yourself

The spiritual contamination in our bodies and minds (soul realm) did not enter in overnight. Through sin or through the circumstances of life, a door was opened and—slowly but surely—strongholds, yokes, and bondages took root and began to control certain areas of our lives. These led to demonic oppression.

As we noted earlier, inner healing and deliverance are akin to going through spiritual surgery. Afterward, there is a period of recovery and adjustment. The length of time required to adjust depends largely upon the extent we were infected by the enemy. We become different people in many respects than we were prior to deliverance and inner healing. Therefore, the first thing we must do is become reacquainted with ourselves. We will notice that we do not act or react in old ways. Things that previously enticed us no longer hold sway over us.

But this is only the beginning. Many changes will come in the days ahead that others will notice as well. The most important change is that we begin to regain control of specific areas of our lives. This means new responsibilities for our attitudes and actions that may take getting used to. During this critical adjustment period it is possible for certain unforeseen problems to develop through no fault of our own. It is necessary that we carefully monitor ourselves for any unusual attitudes and/or actions, although these should be exceptions rather than the rule.

Throughout the Bible, there are many things symbolic of Christ. Because Satan wants to counterfeit what Jesus has done, he has also chosen things that symbolically represent him. We must understand that, in the spirit world, we are considered to be owned by that which we identify with, such as objects, personal possessions, and spiritual loyalty. For example, if through ignorance we have allowed detestable objects into our homes, they must be removed in order to bar legal entry of any related demonic spirits that want to inhabit our lives.[4]

Terminating Unwholesome Relationships

Another step we need to take is to terminate all sinful relationships.

"Be ye not unequally yoked with unbelievers: for what fellowship hath righteousness with unrighteousness? and what communion hath light with darkness?" (2 Corinthians 6:14).

Unfortunately, many Christians believe Paul was referring only to spouses; but this is not true. In verse 17 he continues:

"Wherefore come out from among them, and be ye separate."

He did not say come out from him or her, but from among them, meaning all unhealthy relationships that affect our relationships with the Lord. Suffice it to say, if we are not yet married, we should not become unequally yoked with unbelievers. However, Paul did not mean we are to leave our spouses if we are married to unbelievers.[5] The Bible is not a book of friendly suggestions; it is the standard by which we live and obey.

Warfare

To help maintain our inner healing and deliverance, it is necessary to recognize and deal with the demonic attacks as they occur. This is accomplished by exercising our authority over Satan and his demons in the same manner authority was exercised over them during ministry sessions. Here are several different commands that can be used in any situation by yourself or spoken over someone whom the Lord has burdened you to intercede for:

- Satan, in the name of Jesus, I command the forces of evil (which are my enemies according to the Word) to hereafter be at peace with me.
- Satan, in the name of Jesus, I break and bind the forces of evil from interfering with my marriage.
- In the name of Jesus, I come against the strongholds Satan has erected in my mind. I cast down those strongholds and every high thing in my mind that exalts itself against the knowledge of God.[6] I bind my mind to obedience to Christ. I loose it to be reconciled to God.
- Satan, in the name of Jesus, I command the forces of evil to flee from my church and from my pastor's ministry.

- Satan, in the name of Jesus, I come against your attacks, and bind and break the forces of evil from interfering with my prayer life and my relationship with Jesus.

We suggest engaging in spiritual warfare by using the commands as they are written, unless it is necessary to modify one of them for a particular need. After you have repeated the command several times, allow the Holy Spirit to take over and lead in the way he wishes. We don't need to be timid; we have authority and now know how to combat the enemy.[7]

Witnessing to Others

There is power in our words. Whenever we witness by sharing our personal testimonies or through our treatment of others, we proclaim to the powers of darkness that Jesus is Lord. We should look for God-given opportunities to tell others about our inner healing and deliverance experiences. There are three reasons for this:

1. Our witness adds permanence and strength to what we have experienced.
2. Our testimonies may well be what causes someone to seek the same kind of help.
3. God wants us to witness.[8] He wants to speak through us to reach others, just as he reached us through someone else. However, we should refrain from giving specific details. We give glory to Jesus by simply sharing about his delivering power in our lives and our newfound freedom.

Helpful Hints

The importance of the forty-day period following inner healing and deliverance must be stressed again. It is crucial to maintaining our freedom. Our spiritual equilibrium may be off somewhat, or our body might be sore, but there will be an overriding sense of peace and quietness in our spirit, soul, and body. Everyone reacts a little differently. However, the peace will wear off after a few days. When this happens, some people think they have "lost" their freedom. This is not the case. Instead, the peace has become a part of our lives, and we have subconsciously accepted it as such. We are moving on to a deeper level of life with Christ.

Here are some practical things that we can do for ourselves in the days following our deliverance and inner healing:

- Take some good vitamins and eat lots of protein to help our bodies recover physically.
- Avoid counterattacks, such as arguments and fights, over the next few days. The devil wants to steal what God has done in our lives.
- Practice repentance, not just confession of sin. Deliverance doesn't remove sin; repentance does.
- Make a decision to change. Some struggles are habits and patterns; not everything is a demon.
- Avoid friends and activities that can adversely affect our freedom. Use wisdom with family. After deliverance, some people want to separate from all unsaved people and isolate themselves with God. Remember, Jesus ate with prostitutes and tax collectors, and was still close to the Father.
- Anoint our pets and homes—every opening, all doors and windows, and any fireplaces—with oil. Drive out demons, evil spirits, and human spirits over the next week.[9]
- Stay committed to a local church and get involved, including becoming a tithing member.
- Commit to daily maintenance. Spend time with God for a minimum of one hour and fifteen minutes per day for forty days, except for Sunday when going to church. For example, if you don't have a regular routine, you can spend fifteen minutes in praise and worship daily, fifteen minutes praying in the Spirit, five minutes in quiet time, ten minutes in intercession and warfare prayer, fifteen minutes in Bible study, and fifteen minutes writing in a journal. These times can be interspersed throughout the day. They are filling the void that was created during your inner healing and deliverance, leaving no room for the enemy to regain entry.

Personal Responsibility

After receiving spiritual freedom, we have a responsibility to keep it.

"Stand fast therefore in the liberty wherewith Christ hath made us free, and be not entangled again with the yoke of bondage" (Galatians 5:1).

The only way we become free is when God makes us free. The only way we can stay free is if we stand fast. Some people try to pass on to God the responsibilities that are rightfully theirs.

God is a delivering God, a powerful God, and he will move in our lives and do the miraculous. But many who experience the glorious and miraculous fall back to old ways over time. We are convinced that, according to the Word of God, this is not the way he intended. Instead, we must hold fast to our faith and the responsibilities God has given us. It is up to us to make sure there are no known "cracks, holes, or openings" that develop in our lives, giving the enemy legal access. Inner healing and deliverance are real! But if we go back to our old ways, they will lose their effect.

There are times when the powers and works of darkness become so strong that it takes a dynamic work of the Spirit to break these strongholds. Inner healing and deliverance are tools that God gives us to set us free. But we have to be mature enough to walk out what God has done for us. We need to walk with Jesus *daily*. We must fill our minds with the Word of God. Filling our hearts and minds with good things will help us maintain the victory Jesus has given us. We don't eliminate darkness in a room by opening the windows and doors and pushing the darkness out. We eliminate darkness by turning on the light—the light of God's Word and the presence of the Holy Spirit.

We must be steadfast in reading the Bible, praying, worshipping, and attending church. Keeping our minds on him gives us peace.[10] When God's peace rests in our hearts, we become more sensitive to his voice, and he can direct our paths in the ways of righteousness.

The Aftermath

When a demon is cast out, it will try to reclaim its territory. We must not be fooled into thinking the battle is over after receiving inner healing and deliverance. Receiving ministry is only the first step; we have to prove to the demon(s) that we are standing fast in our victory. Sometimes the battle is fought and won by simply "standing our ground."[11] We must guard against discouragement—against allowing the enemy to guilt-trip us into thinking God has not done anything on our behalf. The enemy comes to "steal, kill, and destroy," but Jesus has come to give us abundant life.[12]

> *We eliminate darkness by turning on the light—the light of God's Word and the presence of the Holy Spirit.*

Satan will have us believe that the battle rages in the same areas because we have done something wrong. Demons will try to convince us they have come back into our lives. Nothing can be further from the truth. We must refuse their lies and deny their fiery darts aimed at our thoughts. The battle rages because they are *trying* to come back into our lives. They may try to afflict us with the same physical, mental, or emotional symptoms we previously had.

When the enemy tries to come in "like a flood" we must raise up a standard in our lives by standing on God's Word, rebuking the devil, and submitting to God. Then the devil has to flee.[13] Demons most often lie (it's their native tongue) and say they are coming back. They will tell us that we are in even worse shape. But they are now on the *outside* trying to get back in. We are to stand on God's truth and his power to deliver us from all that his Word has promised.

Standing Firm

"Wherefore take unto you the whole armour of God, that ye may be able to withstand in the evil day, and having done all, to stand" (Ephesians 6:13).

Standing in faith and not moving forward or backward can some-times be a hard mission. God's ways of thinking can be hard to understand at times, but they are always in our best interest. We must resist becoming frustrated because we feel we're not moving forward in victory. It is important to understand that standing still and holding our ground is a victory in itself.

Passivity and Laziness

One major problem in keeping demons out after receiving inner healing and deliverance can be the lack of discipline in our thought lives. We must learn how to regain control over our minds by "bringing into captivity every thought to the obedience of Christ."[14] Self-control in following biblical commands—whether we feel like it or not—is a fruit of the Spirit.[15] Reading the Bible and seeking God are commands, not options.

Others may say we cannot control or stop demons. This is a lie from Satan himself! He wants us to become spiritually passive and lazy. The Holy Spirit will help us regain control of our thought lives so we can recognize demonic activity the instant it starts. Everything in our Christian walk is by faith, including receiving inner healing and deliverance. We must not let the devil lie to us! The fruit in our lives give testimony to the freeing power of the Holy Spirit. We are to be guided by the Word and the Holy Spirit within us.

One of the best ways of retraining our minds is through Scripture memorization. In fact, we recommend this for everyone after receiving inner healing and deliverance. It overcomes the mind's passivity. The mind is like a muscle: It grows "flabby" with lack of use and grows strong with constant work. Retraining it can be just as painful as retraining a flabby muscle in an out-of-shape body. However, it won't take long before we have developed sound minds once again.

Defeated Christians

There are many who cannot live the Christian life with consistency and productivity. Often this is due to past hurts, oppression, curses, or sins that come about because of disobedience or because of the environment in which we were raised. Jesus said that, "The thief cometh not, but for to steal, and to kill, and destroy: I am come that they might have life, and that they might have it more abundantly" (John 10:10). In contrast to Satan's actions, Jesus says, "The Spirit of the Lord is upon me, because He hath anointed Me to preach the gospel to the poor; he hath sent me to heal the brokenhearted, to preach deliverance to the captives, and recovering of sight to the blind, to set at liberty them that are bruised, To preach the acceptable year of the Lord" (Luke 4:18-19).

During inner healing and deliverance, the minister uses God-given authority and the power of the Holy Spirit to set the captives at liberty, free the oppressed, and heal the brokenhearted.

- Heal the brokenhearted: Many believers are prevented from living according to the Word of God because of bruises and hurts they have received. The circumstances of life and decisions made in reaction to them cause spiritual wounds that are contained in memories. These become binding fetters and chains.
- Deliverance to the captives: Ancestral inheritance plays a major role in determining what our lives will be like. Just as we inherit physical traits, we also inherit certain sins and spiritual attributes, as well as traits that come from our environments. The degree of bondage in our lives can either prevent or shape our responses to the Lord Jesus Christ.
- Set at liberty those who are oppressed: Knowingly or unknowingly, we may have become involved in practices that Satan knows will give him the right to oppress us. Some of these are superstitions, occult practices, books, and movies that are designed to lead us into the occult or away from Christ. We may also come in contact with people who pray to their false gods and pronounce curses, bewitchments, and incantations against us. These are some of the common snares designed by the enemy to put us into bondage and keep us from living Holy Spirit–led lifestyles. These do not determine whether we are born again. However, they can determine the extent to which we are experiencing the abundant life that Jesus promised. The trained, Holy Spirit–empowered minister can identify the causes

of bondage and assist us to set in motion the healing anointing of God, bringing defeat to the demonic spiritual forces and freedom to our lives.

Testimony

Divine Protection

Praise the Lord, Pastors Jerry and Sherill! While attending your inner healing and deliverance seminars, one of the people that ministered to me rebuked car accidents. I didn't think a whole lot about that initially, since I had not had any car accidents in several years, praise God. However, the following Sunday, after church, I was driving down a road and the traffic light up ahead had just turned green. The car in front of me didn't accelerate right away; it just sat there at the light. I slowed down almost to a stop to allow the driver in front of me to accelerate. Well, the driver in back of me apparently didn't realize that a couple of cars ahead of him were not driving at the posted speed rate. I glanced in my rearview mirror and saw, to my shock, that the driver was about to plow right into the back of my car. I didn't have time to think, blow the horn, call on Jesus, or anything! I just looked, frozen. All of a sudden, the driver behind me applied brakes and came to a screeching halt—and didn't touch me! I then started praying in the Spirit. My son was in the back seat and I realized that he could have gotten seriously hurt. Then both of us began praising and thanking God for protecting us (and the car!). It was then I remember how that faithful servant prayed for me regarding car accidents.

Thank you for your faithfulness is directing the Inner Healing and Deliverance conferences. They are truly lifesavers.

Closing Words

After many years of walking with the Holy Spirit in the ministries of inner healing and deliverance, Dr. Sherill and I offer some final words of advice:

Inner healing and deliverance are very real—but they are not a "cure-all." They are both part of an ongoing process of sanctification in our lives. We caution against labeling everything as a demon or blaming past wounds for all of our present behaviors. When a Christian becomes fascinated by demon spirit behavior—how they are grouped in activity and how they operate—there is a subtle enticement to keep one's eyes upon the satanic kingdom instead of on our Lord Jesus Christ. When the disciples became thrilled that demons were subject unto them, Jesus told them to rejoice that their names were written in heaven instead.[16] This is still good advice to the Church today.

We have noticed that many who write on demon spirits attribute things to demon powers that are actually the *choice*, *will*, or *actions* of people who do not want to resist the flesh or their Adamic inheritance (i.e. sin nature) and follow the Holy Spirit in transforming their lives. Remember, demons cannot do anything to us unless we give them legal entry through sin.

Inner healing is healing in the soul and spirit realms. Deliverance is the casting out of actual demonic beings and personalities that have invaded the human body and soul and express themselves through individuals. So be careful what you read and believe. You will notice in the Word that the disciples did not spend all their time "delivering" each other. Instead, they were involved in taking the Good News to those who had never heard of it.

Christians sometimes latch onto deliverance because they think it will be a quick way to get out of a difficult situation. However, daily decisions to change habits and patterns, and crucifying one's flesh, are even more important—and these are not demonic. Be careful what you read, listen to, and absorb about inner healing and deliverance.

The best way for us to learn about the demonic world is to be full of the Spirit through a relationship with Jesus, continually reading and studying the Word, and making sure that what we practice is in line with examples in the Bible. For example, we do not have to take authority over a demon just because we know of its presence. Paul exemplified this in the book of Acts. When the girl came crying after him "he waited many days" until it was the right time.[17] Like Paul, we need to take the whole counsel of God into consideration. When we are open to God, with or without experience in inner healing and deliverance, he will teach us and tell us exactly what to do in that moment.

We need to follow ministers, pastors, and teachers who display the fruit of the Spirit in their ministries. Not by what people say or think but by "their fruits ye shall know them."

We can deal with past hurts and wounds, and our broken hearts, through inner healing. We can deal with the bondages, oppressions, and demon spirits—and see the captives set free—through deliverance. However, it is up to us to change our mindsets, response patterns, lifestyles, and habits in order to walk in freedom. If these are not changed, we will be subject to greater bondage and deeper wounds as the negative cycles reclaim our lives. Only by submitting to the Holy Spirit can we see permanent change.

If the freedom gained through inner healing and deliverance is not followed by a willingness to change our lifestyles, our freedom will offer only "temporary relief."

This is called reality!

Chapter 16 The Aftermath

1 – Luke 4:13
2 – Psalm 23:3
3 – James 1:13-15
4 – Acts 19:18-19; Deuteronomy 7:26
5 – 1 Corinthians 7:13-15
6 – 1 Corinthians 10:3-6
7 – We suggest that you read *Prayers that Rout Demons*, by John Echardt, Charisma House, 2008.
8 – Matthew 28:18-20
9 – Exodus 40:9
10 – Isaiah 26:3; Romans 8:6; Philippians 4:7; 2 Thessalonians 3:16
11 – 1 Corinthians 16:13; Ephesians 6:13
12 – John 10:10
13 – James 4:7
14 – 2 Corinthians 10:3-5
15 – Galatians 5:23
16 – Luke 10:20
17 – Acts 16:16-18

APPENDIX 1

Scriptures on the Blood, Authority of the Believer, Forgiveness, and the Delivering Power of God

Colossians 2:15 – And having spoiled principalities and powers, he made a shew of them openly, triumphing over them in it.

Matthew 16:19 – And I will give unto thee the keys of the kingdom of heaven: and whatsoever thou shalt bind on earth shall be bound in heaven: and whatsoever thou shalt loose on earth shall be loosed in heaven.

Daniel 6:27 – He delivereth and rescueth, and he worketh signs and wonders in heaven and in earth, who hath delivered Daniel from the power of the lions.

Psalm 18:17 – He delivered me from my strong enemy, and from them which hated me: for they were too strong for me.

Psalm 34:7 – "The angel of the Lord encampeth round about them that fear him, and delivereth them.

Psalm 44:5 – Through thee will we push down our enemies: through thy name will we tread them under that rise up against us.

Psalm 91:3 – Surely he shall deliver thee from the snare of the fowler, and from the noisome pestilence.

Jeremiah 1:8 – Be not afraid of their faces: for I am with thee to deliver thee, saith the Lord.

Romans 16:20 – And the God of peace shall bruise Satan under your feet shortly.

Revelation 12:7-12 – And there was war in heaven: Michael and his angels fought against the dragon; and the dragon fought and his angels, And prevailed not; neither was their place found any more in heaven. And the great dragon was cast out, that old serpent, called the Devil, and Satan, which deceiveth the whole world: he was cast out into the earth, and his angels were cast out with him. And I heard a loud voice saying in heaven, Now is come salvation, and strength, and the kingdom of our God, and the power of his Christ: for the accuser of our brethren is cast down, which accused them before our God day and night. And they overcame him by the blood of the Lamb, and by the word of their testimony; and they loved not their lives unto the death. Therefore rejoice, ye heavens, and ye that dwell in them. Woe to the inhabiters of the earth and of the sea! for the devil is come down unto you, having great wrath, because he knoweth that he hath but a short time.

Revelation 20:10 – And the devil that deceived them was cast into the lake of fire and brimstone, where the beast and the false prophet are, and shall be tormented day and night for ever and ever.

Revelation 1:18 – I am He that liveth, and was dead; and, behold, I am alive for evermore, Amen; and have the keys of hell and of death.

Revelation 15:3-4 – And they sing the song of Moses the servant of God, and the song of the Lamb, saying, Great and marvelous are thy works, Lord God Almighty; just and true are thy ways, thou King of saints. Who shall not fear thee, O Lord, and glorify thy name? for thou only art holy: for all nations shall come and worship before thee; for thy judgments are made manifest.

Revelation 17:14 – These shall make war with the Lamb, and the Lamb shall overcome them: for he is Lord of lords, and King of kings: and they that are with Him are called, and chosen, and faithful.

Revelation 18:2 – And he cried mightily with a strong voice, saying, Babylon the great is fallen, is fallen, and is become the habitation of devils, and the hold of every foul spirit, and a cage of every unclean and hateful bird.

Isaiah 43:25 – I, yes, I alone am he who blots away your sins for my own sake and will never think of them again (Living Bible).

Psalm 32:1-2 – What happiness for those whose guilt has been forgiven? What joys when sins are covered over! What relief for those who have confessed their sins and God has cleared their record (Living Bible).

Romans 8:1 – So there is now no condemnation awaiting those who belong to Christ Jesus (Living Bible).

Revelation 19:11-16 – And I saw heaven opened, and behold a white horse; and he that sat upon him was called Faithful and True, and in righteousness he doth judge and make war. His eyes were as a flame of fire, and on his head were many crowns; and he had a name written, that no man knew, but he himself. And he was clothed with a vesture dipped in blood: and his name is called the Word of God. And the armies which were in heaven followed him upon white horses, clothed in fine linen, white and clean. And out of his mouth goeth a sharp sword, that with it he should smite the nations: and he shall rule them with a rod of iron: and he treadeth the winepress of the fierceness and wrath of Almighty God. And he hath on his vesture and on his thigh a name written, KING OF KINGS AND LORD OF LORDS.

Ephesians 1:7 – So overflowing is his kindness towards us that he took away all our sins through the blood of his Son, by whom we are saved. (Living Bible).

Titus 3:5 – Then he saved us, not because we were good enough to be saved but because of his kindness and pity, by washing away our sins and giving us the new joy of the indwelling Holy Spirit (Living Bible).

Hebrews 1:3 – He is the one who died to cleanse us and clear our record of all sin (Living Bible).

Hebrews 10:17 – I will remember their sins and misdeeds no more (Revised Standard Version).

John 8:11 – Neither do I condemn thee: go, and sin no more.

2 Timothy 4:18 – And the Lord shall deliver me from every evil work, and will preserve me unto his heavenly kingdom: to whom be glory for ever and ever.

Mark 16:17-18 – And these signs shall follow them that believe; In my name shall they cast out devils; they shall speak with new tongues. They shall take up serpents; and if they drink any deadly thing, it shall not hurt them; they shall lay hands on the sick, and they shall recover.

Luke 10:17-20 – And the seventy returned again with joy, saying, Lord, even the devils are subject unto us through thy name. And he said unto them, I beheld Satan as lightning fall from heaven. Behold, I give unto you power to tread on serpents and scorpions, and over all the power of the enemy: and nothing shall by any means hurt you. Notwithstanding in this rejoice not, that the spirits are subject unto you.

Luke 11:20 – But if I with the finger of God cast out devils ... .

Matthew 10:1 – And when he had called unto him his twelve disciples, he gave them power against unclean spirits, to cast them out, and to heal all manner of sickness and all manner of disease.

Matthew 18:18 – Verily I say unto you, Whatsoever ye shall bind on earth shall be bound in heaven: and whatsoever ye shall loose on earth shall be loosed in heaven.

1 John 3:8 – For this purpose the Son of God was manifested, that he might destroy the works of the devil.

Genesis 3:14-15 – And the Lord God said unto the serpent, Because thou hast done this, thou art cursed above all cattle, and above every beast of the field; upon thy belly shalt thou go, and dust shalt thou eat all the days of thy life: And I will put enmity between thee and the woman, and between thy seed and her seed; it shall bruise thy head.

Exodus 14:13-14 – Fear ye not, stand still, and see the salvation of the Lord, which he will shew to you to day….. The Lord shall fight for you, and ye shall hold your peace.

Acts 10:38 – How God anointed Jesus of Nazareth with the Holy Ghost and with power: who went about doing good, and healing all that were oppressed of the devil; for God was with him.

Isaiah 54:17 – No weapon that is formed against thee shall prosper; and every tongue that shall rise against thee in judgment thou shalt condemn. This is the heritage of the servants of the Lord.

2 Samuel 22:2 – And he said, The Lord is my rock, and my fortress, and my deliverer.

Philippians 2:8-11 – And being found in fashion as a man, he humbled himself, and became obedient unto death, even the death of the cross. Wherefore God also hath highly exalted him, and given him a name which is above every name: that at the name of Jesus every knee should bow, of things in heaven, and things in earth, and things under the earth; And that every tongue should confess that Jesus Christ is Lord, to the glory of God the Father.

Revelation 20:1-3 – And I saw an angel come down from heaven, having the key of the bottomless pit and a great chain in his hand. And he laid hold on the dragon, that old serpent, which is the Devil, and Satan, and bound him a thousand years, And cast him into the bottomless pit, and shut him up, and set a seal upon him, that he should deceive the nations no more.

2 Peter 2:4 – For if God spared not the angels that sinned, but cast them down to hell, and delivered them into chains of darkness, to be reserved unto judgment.

Matthew 25:41 – Then shall he say also unto them on the left hand, Depart from me, ye cursed, into everlasting fire, prepared for the devil and his angels.

Jude 6 – And the angels which kept not their first estate, but left their own habitation, he hath reserved in everlasting chains under darkness unto the judgment of the great day.

James 2:19 – Thou believest that there is one God; thou doest well: the devils also believe, and tremble.

James 4:7 – Submit yourselves therefore to God. Resist the devil, and he will flee from you.

1 John 2:13 – I write unto you, young men, because ye have overcome the wicked one. I write unto you little children, because you have known the Father.

Hebrews 2:14 – Forasmuch then as the children are partakers of flesh and blood, he also himself likewise took part of the same; that through death he might destroy him that had the power of death, that is, the devil.

Ephesians 6:11 – Put on the whole armour of God, that ye may be able to stand against the wiles of the devil.

2 Corinthians 1:10 – Who delivered us from so great a death, and doth deliver: in whom we trust that he will yet deliver us.

Colossians 2:10 – And ye are complete in him, which is the head of all principality and power.

2 Corinthians 10:3-5 – For though we walk in the flesh, we do not war after the flesh: (For the weapons of our warfare are not carnal, but mighty through God to the pulling down of strong holds;) Casting down imaginations, and every high thing that exalteth itself against the knowledge of God, and bringing into captivity every thought to the obedience of Christ.

2 Corinthians 2:11 – Lest Satan should get an advantage of us: for we are not ignorant of his devices.

Colossians 1:13 – Who hath delivered us from the power of darkness, and hath translated us into the kingdom of his dear Son.

2 Thessalonians 2:8 – And then shall that Wicked be revealed, whom the Lord shall consume with the spirit of his mouth, and shall destroy with the brightness of his coming.

1 John 4:4 – Ye are of God, little children, and have overcome them: because greater is he that is in you, than he that is in the world.

John 12:31 – Now is the judgment of this world: now shall the prince of this world be cast out.

Luke 13:16 – And ought not this woman, being a daughter of Abraham, whom Satan hath bound, lo, these eighteen years, be loosed from this bond on the sabbath day?

Luke 9:1 – Then he called his twelve disciples together, and gave them power and authority over all devils, and to cure diseases.

Acts 5:16 – There came also a multitude out of the cities round about unto Jerusalem, bringing sick folks, and them which were vexed with unclean spirits: and they were healed every one.

Mark 1:27 – "[F]or with authority commandeth he even the unclean spirits, and they do obey Him.

Mark 1:39 – And he preached in their synagogues throughout all Galilee, and cast out devils.

Mark 1:32, 34 – And at even, when the sun did set, they brought unto him all that were diseased, and them that were possessed with devils. … And he healed many that were sick of divers diseases, and cast out many devils.

Matthew 8:16 – When the even was come, they brought unto him many that were possessed with devils: and he cast out the spirits with his word, and healed all that were sick.

Mark 3:14-15 – And he ordained twelve, that they should be with him, and that he might send them forth to preach, And to have power to heal sicknesses, and to cast out devils.

Mark 6:12-13 – And they went out, and preached that men should repent. And they cast out many devils, and anointed with oil many that were sick, and healed them.

Luke 4:36 – And they were all amazed, and spake among themselves, saying, What a word is this! for with authority and power he commandeth the unclean spirits, and they come out.

Luke 6:18-19 – And they that were vexed with unclean spirits: and they were healed. And the whole multitude sought to touch him: for there went virtue out of him, and healed them all.

Luke 7:21 – And in that same hour he cured many of their infirmities and plagues, and of evil spirits; and unto many that were blind he gave sight.

John 8:44 – Ye are of your father the devil, and the lusts of your father ye will do. He was a murderer from the beginning, and abode not in the truth, because there is no truth in him. When he speaketh a lie, he speaketh of his own: for he is a liar, and the father of it.

John 16:8, 11 – And when he is come, he will reprove the world of sin, and of righteousness, and of judgment: … Of judgment, because the prince of this world is judged.

Luke 13:32 – And he said unto them, Go ye, and tell that fox, Behold, I cast out devils, and I do cures to day and to morrow, and the third day I shall be perfected.

Matthew 17:18 – And Jesus rebuked the devil; and he departed out of him: and the child was cured from that very hour.

Matthew 12:22 – Then was brought unto him one possessed with a devil, blind, and dumb: and he healed him.

Luke 9:42 – And Jesus rebuked the unclean spirit, and healed the child, and delivered him again to his father.

Luke 4:41 – And devils also came out of many, crying out.

Acts 8:7 – For unclean spirits, crying with loud voice, came out of many that were possessed with them: and many taken with palsies, and that were lame, were healed.

Mark 3:11 – And unclean spirits, when they saw him, fell down before him, and cried, saying, Thou art the Son of God.

Mark 6:7 – And he called unto him the twelve, and began to send them forth by two and two; and gave them power over unclean spirits.

1 Peter 3:22 – Who is gone into heaven, and is on the right hand of God; angels and authorities and powers being made subject unto him.

Matthew 28:18 – And Jesus came and spake unto them, saying, All power is given unto me in heaven and in earth.

Revelation 11:15 – The kingdoms of this world are become the kingdoms of our Lord, and of his Christ; and he shall reign for ever and ever.

1 Samuel 17:26, 29 – Who is this uncircumcised Philistine, that he should defy the armies of the living God? ... Is there not a cause?

1 Samuel 17:45 – Then said David to the Philistine, Thou comest to me with a sword, and with a spear, and with a shield: but I come to thee in the name of the Lord of hosts, the God of the armies of Israel, whom thou hast defied.

1 Samuel 17:46-47 – This day will the Lord deliver thee into mine hand; and I will smite thee, and take thine head from thee; and I will give the carcases of the host of the Philistines this day unto the fowls of the air, and to the wild beasts of the earth; that all the earth may know that there is a God in Israel. And all this assembly shall know that the Lord saveth not with sword and spear: for the battle is the LORD's and he will give you into our hands.

Hebrews 9:12 – Neither by the blood of goats and calves, but by his own blood he entered in once into the holy place, having obtained eternal redemption for us.

Matthew 26:28 – For this is my blood of the new testament, which is shed for many for the remission of sins.

Romans 5:9 – Much more then, being now justified by his blood, we shall be saved from wrath through him.

Ephesians 1:7 – In whom we have redemption through his blood, the forgiveness of sins, according to the riches of his grace.

Colossians 1:14, 20 – In whom we have redemption through his blood, even the forgiveness of sins: ... And, having made peace through the blood of his cross, by him to reconcile all things unto himself; by him, I say, whether they be things in earth, or things in heaven.

Hebrews 10:19 – Having therefore, brethren, boldness to enter into the holiest by the blood of Jesus.

Hebrews 13:12 – Wherefore Jesus also, that he might sanctify the people with his own blood, suffered without the gate.

Revelation 1:5-6 – Unto him that loved us, and washed us from our sins in his own blood, And hath made us kings and priests unto God and his Father; to him be glory and dominion for ever and ever.

Revelation 7:14 – And he said to me, These are they which came out of great tribulation, and have washed their robes, and made them white in the blood of the Lamb.

Exodus 15:3, 6 – The LORD is a man of war: The LORD is his name. ... Thy right hand, O LORD, is become glorious in power: thy right hand, O LORD, hath dashed in pieces the enemy.

Exodus 9:16 – And in very deed for this cause have I raised thee up, for to shew in thee my power; and that my name may be declared throughout all the earth.

Leviticus 26:8 – And five of you shall chase an hundred, and an hundred of you shall put ten thousand to flight: and your enemies shall fall before you by the sword.

Deuteronomy 33:27 – The eternal God is thy refuge...and He shall thrust out the enemy from before thee; and shall say, Destroy them.

Joshua 21:44 – The Lord delivered all their enemies into their hand.

Job 33:28 – He will deliver his soul from going into the pit, and his life shall see the light.

Isaiah 41:10-12 – Fear thou not; for I am with thee: be not dismayed; for I am thy God: I will strengthen thee; yea, I will help thee; yea, I will uphold thee with the right hand of my righteousness. Behold, all they that were incensed against thee shall be ashamed and confounded ... and they that strive with thee shall perish. ... they that war against thee shall be as nothing, and as a thing of nought.

APPENDIX 2

Manifestations of Spirits Leaving in a Biblical Way

Mark 15:37 – And Jesus cried with a loud voice, and gave up the ghost [Spirit] (Matthew 27:50; Luke 23:46; John 19:30, brackets added).

Mark 15:39 – And when the centurion, which stood over against him, saw that he so cried out, and gave up the ghost, he said, Truly this man was the Son of God.

Mark 1:25-26 – And Jesus rebuked him, saying, Hold thy peace, and come out of him. And when the unclean spirit had torn him, and cried with a loud voice, he came out of him.

Mark 1:26 – At that the evil spirit screamed and convulsed the man violently and left him (Living Bible).

Mark 1:26 – And the unclean spirit, convulsing him and crying with a loud voice, came out of him (Revised Version).

Mark 1:26 – At this the evil spirit convulsed the man, let out a loud scream and left him (Philips Modern English).

Mark 1:26 – The evil spirit shook the man violently and came out of him with a shriek (NIV).

Mark 1:26 – The evil spirit shook the man hard, gave a loud scream, and came out of him (The English Version).

Luke 4:41 – And devils also came out of many, crying out, and saying, Thou art Christ the Son of God. And he rebuking them suffered them not to speak: for they knew that he was Christ.

Luke 4:35 – And Jesus rebuked him, saying, Hold thy peace, and come out of him. And when the devil had thrown him in the midst, he came out of him, and hurt him not.

Acts 8:7 – For unclean spirits, crying with loud voice, came out of many that were possessed with them: and many taken with palsies, and that were lame, were healed.

Acts 8:7 – Many evil spirits were cast out, screaming as they left their victims (The Living Bible).

Acts 8:7 – With loud cries evil spirits came out. (Philips Modern English).

Acts 8:7 – With shrieks evil spirits came out of many. (NIV).

Mark 9:17-26 – And one of the multitude answered and said, Master, I have brought unto thee my son, which hath a dumb spirit; And wheresoever he taketh him, he teareth him: and he foameth, and gnasheth with his teeth, and pineth away: and I spake to thy disciples that they should cast him out; and they could not. He answered him, and saith, O faithless generation, how long shall I be with you? how long shall I suffer you? bring him unto me. And they brought him unto him: and when he saw him, straightway the spirit tare him; and he fell on the ground, and wallowed foaming. And he asked his father, How long is it ago since this came unto him? And he said, Of a child. And ofttimes it hath cast him into the fire, and into the waters, to destroy him: but if thou canst do any thing, have compassion on us, and help us. Jesus said unto him, If thou canst believe, all things are possible to him that believeth. And straightway the father of the child cried out, and said with tears, Lord, I believe; help thou mine unbelief. When Jesus saw that the people came running together, he rebuked the foul spirit, saying unto him, Thou dumb and deaf spirit, I charge thee, come out of him, and enter no more into him. And the spirit cried, and rent him sore, and came out of him: and he was as one dead; insomuch that many said, He is dead.

Mark 9:26 – The spirit gave a loud scream and after a dreadful convulsion left him. (Philips Modern English).

Mark 9:26 – And after crying out and convulsing him terribly, it came out, and the boy was like a corpse (Revised Standard Version).

Mark 9:26 – The spirit shrieked, convulsed him violently and came out (NIV).

Mark 9:26 – Then throwing the boy into violent convulsions, it came out shouting. (Jerusalem Bible).

Mark 9:27-29 – But Jesus took him by the hand, and lifted him up; and he arose. And when he was come into the house, his disciples asked him privately, Why could we not cast him out? And he said unto them, This kind can come forth by nothing, but by prayer and fasting.

Mark 5:8-9 – For he said unto him, Come out of the man, thou unclean spirit. And he asked him, What is thy name? And he answered, saying, My name is Legion: for we are many.

TARE/RENT Greek = spasmodic contraction, to convulse with epilepsy; to convulse violently; root word in Greek is the verb *to draw out*. Note: The modern day word "epilepsy" comes from these words.

APPENDIX 3

Prayers of Renunciation

RELEASE FROM THE INIQUITIES OF THE PAST

We acknowledge Lord, our wickedness and the wickedness and iniquities of our fathers, for we have sinned against You. We ask that You remove from us and from our children the consequences of our and our fathers' iniquities. In the name of Jesus, we cast out any familiar spirit attached to the family line, breaking harmful generational ties of destructive patterns in family lines, physical weakness, attitudes, spiritual influences, rebellion from God, occult practices, and all doubt and unbelief. We apply by faith the cross of Jesus and the blood of Jesus between each generation, between me and my children, between me and my husband/wife, between me and my parents, and between me and my grandparents on both sides of my family line. We ask You, Lord, to close the doors and seal them with Your precious blood.

CURSES

In the name of Jesus, I come before You, Father, and I break any and all curses of and caused by sexual perversion, witchcraft, sorcery, or charmed by black magic, whether they have been spoken over, about, placed or prayed in or out of me (or my family) or that are inherited. I come against curses and command their powers and effects to be broken and to depart from me. I bind and rebuke any and all curses with the blood of Jesus and in the name of Jesus. I loose any associated and affiliated demons because of these curses from their orders, networks, systems and groupings; and I break their orders and assignments in the all-powerful name of Jesus. I now break any curses I may have put on anyone else and I release them in the name of Jesus. Amen.

VOWS & PROMISES

Father, in the name of Jesus, I now break, of my own free will, all vows of consecration to anyone or anything, such as a church, kingdom, organization, or religion, or through superstition, that may have been made for me, that I have made for others, or that I made for myself. I sever all ties of bondage in these areas by the name of Jesus and by the blood of Jesus. I consecrate myself to You, Father God, alone, to be Your vessel of love, and I thank You. Forgive me, Lord. Amen.

MIND CONTROL

Heavenly Father, in Jesus' name I renounce mind control and ask You to send your Holy Spirit and angels to seal off every door through which mind control is receiving reinforcement, entrance, control, and aid. Block every access with the blood of Jesus. Father, I ask that all spirits in these places from which mind control could draw strength be sealed off. Send angels to break and prevent all communication of such spirits, in the name of the Lord Jesus Christ and by His shed blood. Amen.

SEXUAL SIN

Heavenly Father, I come to You in the name of the Lord Jesus Christ. I renounce and claim freedom in Jesus' name from all filth of a sexual nature that came through my eyes, my ears, my mind or actual participation in this sin. I confess all preoccupation with any passions or lusts that tend to produce sexual sin in my thoughts, mind, or emotions. I confess any and all filthy conversations; obscene or filthy language or jokes; lewd or obscene music, poetry, literature, or art; all pornography; all acts of sodomy, adultery, immorality, fornication, masturbation, homosexuality, lesbianism, prostitution, child molestation, rape, incest, and bestiality, and any and all sexual perversion. I renounce anything of a sexual nature that is contrary to the standard set for believers in the Bible. I also now reclaim all ground I have ever given to Satan in body, soul, or spirit. I dedicate that ground to you, Lord, to be used for your glory alone. I want You to control and empower every area of my life, including all my sexual powers, that from now on, they might be used according to Your will. I give you, Lord Jesus, my affections, emotions, and desires; and I request that they might be motivated and controlled by your Holy Spirit. Amen.

COMMITMENT

Lord Jesus, today I commit my life completely to You, spirit, soul, and body. I ask that You bend, break, and mold me into the person that You want me to be. Lord, teach me to trust in You and to live and walk by faith. Satan, I come against you and all the hosts of hell and reject everything you would have for me. I refuse all the snares, pits, and traps you have set to draw me away from the Lord Jesus Christ. I rebuke you, Satan, and all your hosts in the name of the Lord Jesus Christ. Father, I ask for your best in my life today and that your will and purposes be done in and through me. I also ask that You keep me in Your perfect will and make me a yielded vessel for Your work today. Amen.

BLOOD COVENANT

Through the blood of Jesus I am redeemed out of the hand of the devil. Through the blood of Jesus all my sins are forgiven. The blood of Jesus Christ, God's Son, is cleansing me now from all sin. Through the blood of Jesus I am justified, made righteous, just as if I had never sinned. Through the blood of Jesus I am sanctified, made holy, set apart for God. My body is a temple for the Holy Spirit, redeemed, cleansed, and sanctified by the blood of Jesus. I belong to the Lord Jesus Christ, God's Son, spirit, soul, and body. His blood protects me from all evil. Because of the blood of Jesus, Satan has no more power over me, no more place in me. I renounce him and his hosts completely and I declare them to be my enemies. I command them to leave me now, according to the Word of God and in the name of Jesus. I place the blood of Jesus on my doorposts; I draw the bloodline of Jesus around myself, my family, my friends, and my possessions and properties.

STUBBORNNESS & REBELLION

Father, I come to You now confessing that I have been rebellious, disobedient, stubborn, obstinate, and many other things You have forbidden. I now renounce and forsake these sins and ask for and receive Your forgiveness and deliverance, in Jesus' name, from these and all connected, related, and resulting spirits.

DOMINATION

In the name of Jesus I now renounce, break, and loose myself from all demonic subjection to my mother, father, grandparents, or any other human being, living or dead, that has ever in the past or is now dominating or controlling me in any way contrary to the will of God. I thank You, Lord, for setting me free. I also repent and ask You to forgive me if I am now or have in the past dominated or controlled anyone the wrong way.

PRIDE, DOUBT, & UNBELIEF

Father, I come to You in the name of Jesus. I know that pride is an abomination to you; that a haughty look, a lying tongue, hands that shed innocent blood, a heart that devises wicked imaginations, feet that are swift in running to mischief, a false witness that speaketh lies, and he that sows discord among brethren are seven things that the Lord hates and are an abomination unto God (Proverbs 6:16-19).

Father, I renounce these and turn away from them. I humble myself before You and come to You as a little child. Father, I renounce unbelief and doubt as sin, and I ask You to forgive me for entertaining them. I refuse to let these spirits operate in my mind, my life, or my walk.

ATTITUDE PRAYER

God, I know that You are holy and cannot sin. You do all things well. My attitude toward You has been, at times, one of questioning and bitterness. This is sin. I repent of it. Wash it out of me with your blood.

I realize that all evil comes from Satan, not from You. Forgive me for blaming You for any of the works of the enemy. I can and do trust You. I know all things do work together for my good. Father, I love You and pray this in Jesus' name.

OCCULT RENUNCIATION

Jesus, I confess that through ignorance or willfulness I have sought supernatural experiences apart from You. I bind, rebuke, and renounce all spirits of denial. I have disobeyed Your Word, and I ask you to help me as I renounce all these things. Cleanse me in spirit, soul, and body, I pray. Satan, I close any door that I may have opened to You through contact with the occult. I renounce all contact with the occult. Forgive me, Lord. Amen.

PSYCHIC HEREDITY RENUNCIATION

In the name of Jesus I renounce, break, and loose myself from all psychic heredity, demonic holds, psychic powers, bondages, physical or mental illness, or curses put upon me as the result of sins, transgressions, iniquities, occult, or psychic involvements of myself, my parents, my ancestors, my spouse or ex-spouses, their parents or their ancestors. I thank You, Lord, for setting me free.

POWER & WITCHCRAFT

Lord Jesus, I remove and relinquish all of my ability, powers, control, and communication with the evil spirit world; and I ask You, Lord Jehovah, to use your word to divide between my soul and spirit. Lord, let me not control my own human spirit, but I ask You to take complete control of my human spirit. I bind, rebuke, and renounce all power spirits. Lord, I will not use witchcraft even to protect myself. Lord, my conscious, subconscious, and unconscious mind I ask You to sever from my human spirit so You can control all of me. I release and will my spirit to be totally under the mastership and Lordship of Jesus Christ.

PASSIVITY

Heavenly Father, please forgive my laziness and lack of diligence in seeking and spending good quality time with You on a daily basis. Forgive me for allowing excuses, rationalization, and the busyness of this life to overtake me.

APPENDIX 4

Additional Testimonies

Over the years that Dr. Sherill and I have been involved with deliverance and personal healing, we have received thousands of letters testifying of the freedom people have received while giving all glory to the One who set them free—Jesus Christ. The following testimonies are samples of those we have received, along with the ones you have already read.

Peace that Passes all Understanding

Dear Drs. Jerry & Sherrill Piscopo, Rev. Sandra Rice, and all the wonderful people at Evangel Christian Churches,

Wow! What a weekend! I am still walking ten feet off the ground and experiencing the most *peace* that I have had in a long time, maybe ever.

How do I say "thank you"? Thank you for showing me what a church body should be like. I felt like I was back with Peter and Paul and a part of the church from the book of Acts. Everyone that I came in contact with walked in love and unity of spirit, and a true caring for each and every one of us who was there for the deliverance seminar. The dedication, the willingness to share, the eagerness to serve were something that I had never experienced in a church before. I have bragged to ministers, people in my office, and even strangers on the street about this unique body of believers called Evangel.

The workshop was everything I expected and more. Sometimes the flesh tries to war against what was happening, but I have seen wonderful results since I have been back home. My husband says that he sees a different wife, and a friend told me yesterday that I glowed and that my entire countenance had changed. Someone who works for me said, "last week you looked worn out; today you look rested and at peace. You must have had some vacation."

The "icing on the cake" was the Sunday morning service. This should be a requirement after the workshop. Everything comes together, and that is when you realize what a miracle has taken place in your spirit man. The Sunday morning service (for me) was the glue that bonded the inner healing and deliverance experience to my spirit and to my soul. Both were and are on the same wavelength. This is truly a miracle of grace!

Pastor John, thank you for the transportation and your sweet, sweet spirit. Pastor Tom, the praise and worship were awesome. Rev. Rice, the words that you spoke over so many were straight from the throne of grace. Most of all, thank you for your time and dedication to setting people free.

Dr. Piscopo, what can I say. First, if I had any doubts about my affiliation with E.A.C.M., they are dispelled now. You are a man truly after GOD's heart. Your love for people is something that so many pastors, teachers, and so-called children of GOD could take lessons for. THANK YOU!!! Thank you for your passion, your vision, and your tenacity to see it all come together and to completion.

I want to end this by saying that I truly love my family at Evangel Christian Churches and E.A.C.M. Please keep me in your prayers. You are in mine.

A Day Well Remembered

First of all, I would like to thank you all so much for the time you spent with me. It was a day that I will remember the rest of my life. I didn't know there were so many loving people at Evangel! My eyes have seen the light of Jesus Christ. I didn't realize this until I went through Inner Healing and Deliverance. I was reading my Bible with very little understanding at all. I held on to ungodly things. I had very little patience and an attitude problem. But through the help of the seminar workers, my eyes are opened to the Word of Christ Jesus. I have patience now, and I understand God's Word better. It's real; I can feel and hear Him now. I love Jesus Christ my Lord and all of you. Pray for me as I pray for you all.

A Brother's Praise Report

I have been feeling much better since going through the inner healing and deliverance seminar. Before the seminar I was feeling really bound up due to my inability to handle the pressures that I had at work. About a week before the seminar I finally realized in a strong way that I better get my mind on Jesus and get it off the meditation of the sins that I thought would satisfy me. I know that attitude would have eventually gotten me into sin if I didn't change it. Even though some light got through my darkened mind, I knew that my mind was far from being free. At the seminar I was set free!! It has been easier to worship and pray. Since the inner healing and deliverance seminar, I will not say that everything has been going well; but I feel that I had a fresh new start. I have tolerated pressure better and have not had any strong temptations to meditate on sin. I have more time to fight the devil on behalf of other people rather than using the little spiritual strength I had just trying to fight the devil in my own life. I feel that inner healing and deliverance seminars like this are badly needed in the body of Christ. As a body we must be set free to prevent the destruction of our lives. As the glory of God increases on the earth in these last days, the temptations and deceptions of the devil will also increase, so we must be strong and spiritually healthy to fight the devil and do the work of God. There is a lot of work to be done for God in a very short time. Thank You, Jesus, for setting me FREE!!!

Shouts of Joy

Deliverance has really done a big change in my life recently. I was delivered from prostitution and severe drug addiction. I was saved in 1972 but could never have a serious relationship with Jesus because I couldn't stop doing these things. After this first deliverance, which took place at the altar, I got married and started to live a normal Christian life. Close to three years later I was severely attacked by the enemy, and my husband backslid. Here I was with a three-year-old daughter to raise. I thank God I had Pastors Jerry and Sherill to talk to and council with while I was trying to straighten my life out. Although I was given prayer and counseling, the enemy really came in and I started having an unhealthy relationship with a non-Christian man. I knew this was wrong. I was lonesome, and he seemed to be just what I needed; but I knew it was all wrong. I developed a "soul tie" with this man that seemed impossible to break. It was a battle. I attended one of the inner healing and deliverance workshops, and I have been totally set free from this man. My walk with God is much better. Everything is falling into place in my life. Inner healing and deliverance have made such a difference in my walk that I would recommend anyone who is bound up in the things of this world to go through deliverance. IT WILL CHANGE YOUR LIFE!

A Workshop Physical Healing Testimony

During your inner healing and deliverance seminar, I was delivered from the remaining epilepsy in me. One of the workshop ministers called it out, and it did calm down a bit; but now I am completely free—thanks be to God! So now I want to tell you about what it is like to discover over time that the limitations caused by the epilepsy are no longer there. It has been a joy. The form of epilepsy was "atypical myoclonus." Basically it is not found too commonly in adults; it is more like the kind very young infants display from an immature (and growing) central nervous system. Not getting enough sleep was like tempting the epilepsy, so I got very protective about my sleep. While at the seminar, I was scared to scream or get too riled up because it would mean a bad seizure. But since then, I am relearning my body and the new frontiers of activity open to me. It has been a real JOY and fun to discover that I do not have to do any of those protective behaviors anymore. Thank You, Jesus!!

A Recent Testimony

The inner healing and deliverance ministry of Pastors Jerry & Sherill Piscopo was used by the Lord to heal me of some very deep wounds from the past. I had far from an ideal childhood. I grew up in an alcoholic home and suffered much emotional, mental, and physical abuse. Satan is a dirty fighter and made many inroads in my life when I was a small, defenseless child. The Lord had already done a great deal of healing in me before I met Pastors Jerry and Sherill, but there were still barriers between me and God; no amount of prayer and willpower on my part could seem to get me through those barriers. I still had distortions in my mind of what God is like, and I was unable to trust Him as fully as I wanted to. All I could do was throw myself on His mercy and ask for His help, telling Him I would do whatever He showed me to.

Shortly after praying this prayer, I met Drs. Jerry and Sherill. Through their ministry, I discovered that I had repressed many painful and terrifying memories. I have learned where such things as fear, hurt, anxiety, and confusion, too, rooted in my life. I have gone through two seminars now, and strongholds have been torn down each time. In their place, God has put a strength that simply was not there before. To put it another way, the Lord has used the inner healing and deliverance ministry to make great inroads in healing my broken heart. I have observed in myself a new freedom in praising and worshipping God and in telling Him how much I love Him. My prayer life has improved, and I find that I am able to do battle against the evil one more effectively (going on the offensive rather than always being on the defensive).

I am more able to love my enemies and bless those who persecute me. I find myself more able to see things the way God sees them, and because of this I have peace! The anxiety is gone, replaced by a deep assurance that His thoughts toward me are for good and not evil. I am more able to believe that He has everything in my life under control, even if it doesn't always look that way to me. I can't speak for anyone but myself, but I can state without any doubt at all that God has used the Piscopos' ministry to strengthen and bless me in a mighty way.

A Closer Walk

This is the third day since my deliverance, and I do feel the new life and power of Jesus Christ in my spirit. I knew there was new life and refreshing in the Spirit the first time I came to Evangel. I was convinced I was in the right place. As time went on and I heard more about the workshop, I sensed that this would be the next step closer to my Heavenly Father. I knew I needed inner healing for past hurts of many years ago. Gradually the Holy Spirit drew me away from the worldly attractions since the time of my profession of faith and trust in Jesus Christ, my Savior and Lord. I greedily began studying the Word and praised Him. Since the workshop I feel safe and have more confidence. This morning in praise I sang a new song to the Lord. Although the tears still trickle down my cheeks, they were tears of blessing Him. I bless God ... I am blessed, blessed, blessed ... and more blessed than ever before!

Glory to God!

Praise the Lord, Pastors Jerry and Sherill! Where should I start? It's been over a year since I attended my first inner healing and deliverance seminar, after making Evangel my home church. I have been a Spirit-filled believer for almost twenty years and a regular church attendee, and not given over to carnal sins and passions. Once I crawled out of the occult and rededicated my life to Christ in college, I burned all my occult paraphernalia and never looked back. For nearly twenty years I surrounded my life with church service and Christian friends. The years slipped by. However, no matter how much I prayed, certain prayers just weren't getting answered. I flunked five out of ten categories on Derek Prince's "Are You Under a Curse?" test. Also, many strange and unexplainable tragedies dogged my life that I kept hidden under years of church leadership and a successful freelance practice. Yet despite the success in my life, I became convinced I was under a curse and arrived at Evangel's doorstep eager to see if I could be delivered from the enemy's attacks.

During my first deliverance session, I knew I was in trouble when I could feel different spirits popping out of my eyes, like popcorn bursting in a popcorn maker. The experience opened my eyes in many ways to the spiritual reality of demons, even for a dedicated believer like myself. I can't count how many evil spirits left me that day. However, I do remember the next morning sitting in McDonald's having coffee and feeling like I had a hole in my head, an empty space where a mind control spirit had vacated the evening before. As I stirred my coffee, I pondered the reality of what I had just experienced. I recalled how for years I could read people's minds. It had been a great asset counseling and pastoring individuals. The charismatic gift of knowledge I thought I had turned out to be a demonic imposter, an old fortunetelling/divination spirit still attached to my brain that scanned other demons in and around people, obtaining illicit information about individuals from these other spirits, which it then passed on to me. It became clear that demons don't automatically leave once a person gets saved, baptized, or rededicated. The authority and blood of Jesus has to be applied directly to them. They don't give up their territories unless forced to do so! All those charismatic prayer meetings and all the personal laying on of hands in Spirit-filled circles over the years hadn't flushed them out of me, either.

As for detestable objects and curses, I arrived at my first workshop and declared that my whole household of antique furniture had to go. I wasn't getting extreme. I had good reason to believe they were cursed. Unexplainable things would happen in my home. Friends would come over and "suggest" that my grandmother's picture in my bedroom be taken off the wall. The Victorian photo gave them the creeps. To be honest, I could "feel" my grandmother's presence in the home, the same one from which I had inherited most of my furniture from my parents. That gave me the creeps, too. She had been dead for ten years. However, it was only after I was delivered from a curse over my life concerning this grandmother's participation In the *Order of the Eastern Star*—the woman's division of the Masons—that I was sure the furniture had to go.

Right after this curse was broken, my home became infested with beetles. They were everywhere. It was like Egypt. They were on my counters, tables, bathtub, desk; just everywhere. I'd squish them on the floor as I walked, and the sickening odor of their burning bodies infiltrated the home from my living room lamp. I'd open my mouth to talk on the phone and they would zoom in. In my desperation, I went to the local exterminator, and the owner's wife became interested in the sample beetles I had brought to her. She had never seen insects like this before. After careful research, she finally sent them to a department at the University of Michigan that specializes in insects. They couldn't identify them either! The healing and deliverance workshop not only delivered me from demons but broke the occult soul tie between my grandmother and myself that had given the forces of darkness access to my life. After this soul tie was broken, I still had my inherited furniture, but the strange, unexplainable happenings have ceased—and the beetles have disappeared!

Drs. Jerry & Sherill Piscopo, Simon & Trish Presland, book signing party, 2010

Drs. Jerry & Sherill, Evangel Church administrative office, 2008

Spiritual parents, Dr. Emanuele & Shirley Cannistraci, 2007

Piscopo family, 1993

DSM graduation with Dr. Sandra Gay, former senior pastoral assistant, 2003

Doctoral graduation, 2001

Dr. Sherill leading dance and praise at a network
church at which she also preached, 2001

Dr. Jerry preaching in his original church, 1989

Drs. Jerry & Sherill on their wedding day, 1986

Jenna, Bree, Jerry, & Sherill Piscopo, 2011

About Drs. Jerry and Sherill Piscopo

Jerry Piscopo, D. Ministry, D.Div., M.Div., B.B.A., and Sherill Piscopo, D. Ministry, D.Div., M.Div., B.E., are pastors, founders, and/or overseers of the following ministries, schools, and spiritual warfare conference:

- Evangel Christian Church (ECC) and Evangel Ministries International (EMI).
- Evangel Association of Churches and Ministries (EACM), a national and international network of churches, ministries, and ministers. EACM offers ministerial and ministry credentials and covering under its group status 501 (c)3. Complete ministry setup, counsel, and pastoral relationship are available for member churches, ministries, and ministers needing assistance.
- Hosts of Restoration Now, a nightly radio broadcast heard throughout southeast Michigan and southern Ontario, and carried on fifty-two stations throughout the USA.
- Chancellors and deans of Destiny Schools of Ministry (DSM). DSM teaches and equips students in the Word, bringing a balance between an academic and practical approach to ministry.
- Corporate officers of Destiny Christian University.
- Christian Counseling Institute (CCI), a two-year diploma program and four-year bachelors. Through a combination of Christ-centered teachings, counseling principles and techniques, CCI provides solid biblical training for the lay or professional counselor.
- Worship Arts Institute (WAI), a two-year diploma program. WAI's goal is to equip, teach, and develop those who are interested in worship and leading worship at the local church.
- Christian Leadership and Financial Institute (CLFI), a two-year diploma program. CLFI aims to assist in the training and development of those who influence the marketplace.
- Apostles and Prophets Institute (API), a two-year diploma program and four-year Bachelor's degree. API fosters a balanced approach for the apostolic and prophetic gifts and callings while

providing necessary tools and training methods to equip those called to these areas of ministry.

- Chaplain Training Institute (CTI), a two-year diploma program and four-year Bachelor's degree. CTI trains ministers and pastors in the dynamics of chaplaincy, equipping them to respond to disasters, search and rescue, hospitals, prisons, police, and fire departments.
- Hebrew Messianic Christian Institute (HMCI), a two-year diploma program. HMCI specializes in a Messianic perspective of conveying Bible truths with a commitment to the historic, literal interpretation of Scripture and practical insights that teach the Body of Christ about its Jewish roots.
- International Association of Chaplains, an integral part of EACM, credentialing and training chaplains to meet the call of compassionate care outside of the church to needy people in trauma situations of every age, culture, and state of life.
- Spiritual Warfare Conference. For more than twenty-five years, this monthly conference has been a catalyst for changing thousands of lives by setting people free through the ministries of personal healing and deliverance.

All schools are licensed by the state of Michigan and accredited by Accrediting Commission International. Each school provides in-house and distance learning opportunities. For more information concerning any of the above ministries, schools, or conference, contact Evangel Christian Church at 586-773-6568 or on the Web at www.evangel-churches.com. You can also write to:

Drs. Jerry & Sherill Piscopo
28491 Utica Road, Roseville, MI 48066

Acknowledgements

We wish to express our gratitude and appreciation to the following people:

To Drs. Alonzo and Sandra Gay for your years of love, support, and faithfulness.

To Pastors Simon and Trish Presland for making this book "happen" and for all of your love.

To the deliverance and personal healing seminar teams, past and present; you have diligently made the truths of this book produce healing and restoration in countless lives.

To all who have been faithful workers in or have gone through the seminar; may you live free and share God's healing touch on your lives with others.

To our Evangel family; you have supported the vision of deliverance and personal healing for more than twenty-five years.

To the EACM pastors and ministers; you support and share our hearts to see the captive set free and the brokenhearted healed.

To Apostle C and Sister C, "mom and dad," your years of oversight, wisdom, and guidance have been invaluable.

To our two beautiful daughters, Genna and Bree, for your love, patience, and willingness to chase after God with us in times of adversity and victory—you are our joy!

To our Lord Jesus Christ, who makes all things possible; we dedicate our lives to you and the kingdom work you've called us to.

We trust this book has helped deepen your walk with the Lord and given you in-depth understanding into the ministries of personal healing and deliverance. If so, please consider buying a copy of the book and giving it to someone who will benefit from it.

We pray God's richest blessings on your lives as you follow his will and ways.

--Drs. Jerry & Sherill Piscopo

Drs. Jerry and Sherill Piscopo are available to preach, teach, or minister at your church services, conventions, conferences, and workshops. For more information contact:

Evangel Christian Churches
28491 Utica Road, MI, 48066
or call
586-773-6568

The Spiritual Warfare Seminar overseers are available to come to your church to help you implement the ministries of personal healing and deliverance. Please contact Evangel Christian Churches for more information.

Made in the USA
Charleston, SC
06 August 2011